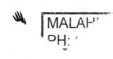
MIRACLES

MIRACLES

AND VISITS FROM
THE AFTERLIFE

EDWARD JEFFRIES

Matador
9 Priory Business Park
Kibworth Beauchamp
Leicestershire LE8 0RX, UK
Tel: (+44) 116 279 2299
Fax: (+44) 116 279 2277
Email: books@troubador.co.uk
Web: www.troubador.co.uk/matador

ISBN 978 1780885 636

British Library Cataloguing in Publication Data.
A catalogue record for this book is available from the British Library.

Foreword

When I look back over my life, I realise that although I have been relatively successful in material things and I have enjoyed myself in many ways, I have not lived a Christian life. Sometimes I have pretended to but it was only on the surface and on Sundays. My first three marriages failed because I nearly always put myself first. In my first marriage, to Jeanette, my job came joint first and I got a lot of satisfaction doing it and enjoyed the large amount of drinking that went with it.

I did my best to try and be a good father, in material ways, but one of my children ran away when only in his early teens. I was away from home a lot, working abroad and leaving them to get on with life in our lovely home.

I had written regularly to report on my activities and when I came home after working nine months in the USA, they did *all* meet me at the airport but when I got home I saw that my wife had another man installed in our house as a 'guest' and our relationship was over. We were soon divorced.

My second wife, Maria, left me because we only had one thing in common and that was a love of wine. We encouraged each other and had parties, but my drinking far exceeded hers and became intolerable. She left, but I don't blame her and I hope she is happier now, wherever she is.

I have now changed. The beginning was a miracle to heal my neck, which was broken.

Then, at a healing service that I was dragged to like a silent donkey, I was healed from alcoholism – believe me, that is some miracle. Then, to even up the score, the asthma that my new partner had was also healed by a miracle in the same church and later she walked up Mount Snowdon in Wales to prove it.

And then there we were: two new people who had both been through suffering, now starting to live a new life together. We enjoyed being involved in church activities together. I sincerely participated in prayer groups. I enjoyed developing our talents together. She started painting and writing while I was working on the farm.

With those miracles, God gave us two people a new start and now we are trying to live our lives as we think Jesus showed us how. Loving God, loving each other and loving ourselves and all of our neighbours.

Chapter 1

Family

When I read the autobiographical book *Memories, Dreams and Reflections* by Dr Carl Jung about 40 years ago, it made a great impression on me. It was really the first time that I had been exposed to serious thinking about life. Then when an interview with Dr Jung by Desmond Wilcox took place on BBC2 television, I was shattered when at the end of the two-hour interview the climax question was – "Dr Jung, do you believe in God?" Jung delayed and tugged at his little pointed beard as he thought, and repeated, "Do I believe in God? Do I believe in God? No," he replied, "I do not believe in God, I *know him*." At that moment I thought it was a stupid reply; how can anyone know God? But now because of my own experiences, I have to say that I do not *believe* in the afterlife, and if Heaven is the place where people live after they cease living in the world that we can touch and see, I do not *believe* in it, I *know* that they exist. In this book I have found it necessary to write about my childhood and my family background as they tend to act like a frame round the picture and to show what a very ordinary life I have lived and what an ordinary person I am and have been.

I only met my great grandfather once, when he came from his home in Derby, where he had been a furniture maker and carpenter, to stay for a few days with us. He was 95 and when I met him he was quite well and mobile. He had a little pointed white beard and he entertained me, at the age of five, by reading me some of the poetry that he had written (I probably didn't know what poetry was then). One of the pieces that he had with him was an acrostic that he had done to promote a new cinema in Derby. As a reward, they had given him a certificate entitling him to two free seats in the cinema every week for the rest of his life.

My father's father was born in Birmingham and he had been a baker most of his life until he retired at the age of 70, when he sold his shop and the bakery business. I remember that he made excellent hand-raised pork pies that were better than any that I have tasted since.

Round about the year 1910, times were hard and

business was difficult. He had heard of the new prosperity in Canada as one of his brothers, Uncle Arthur, had already gone to Newfoundland as a Salvation Army missionary. He had had letters from him with some items of local news. My grandfather, Charlie, decided to go to Canada to look for work. It meant leaving his wife and young son behind but he went off and got a well-paid job, cooking the food for a team of railway construction workers that were working in the wilderness towards Manitoba.

He had written home asking his wife Mary to come and visit him and see for herself what their life could be. She arranged for my father, who was 10, to stay with grandfather's brother Isaac, Uncle Ike and his wife, Auntie Queenie, and off she went to Canada. We will never know what her decision was as she never arrived home. Many weeks later, her husband found out that the ship bringing her home, *The Empress of Ireland*, had been in collision with a Norwegian oil tanker in fog in the Gulf of St Lawrence and she was listed as missing, presumed lost. The St Lawrence River is 17 miles wide at that place and Charlie gave up his work and spent weeks searching the riverbanks on each side, but without finding anything that could be a clue.

He came home and started baking again and my dad stayed with Ike and Queenie. Then Uncle Ike went into the army, into the Royal Flying Corps, and became friendly with another ex-tailor, Jack Cohen, who had trained as a buttonhole maker. His skills with cloth were useful in maintaining the fighting aircraft of that time. That was about 1916. After the war ended in 1918, Ike came home and started tailoring again while Jack was doing quite well selling ex-army surplus canned foods from a handcart around the London markets. He invited Ike to join him, but Ike carried on working very hard as a bespoke tailor. When we were chatting, he told me of this and wondered what life would have been like if he had gone into the barrow business.

By then, Jack was selling tea from the barrow, pushing it as far as Croydon once a week. He bought the tea from a man named Tom Estwood, who shared the same railway arch with him. The tea was good and sold well and other traders wanted to buy it, so they packed it from the tea chest into one-pound bags and had to give the tea a brand name. From their own two names, Tom Estwood and Jack Cohen, they made TESCO. Uncle Ike wondered if Jack Cohen made the right decision, as Jack's trading business grew into the international supermarket company that we know today.

My father was born in 1900 at the baker's shop in Birmingham. That was the last year of the reign of Queen Victoria. He had an uneventful childhood and slowly discovered that he had a very good natural memory. One day, the children in his class at school were taken to Stratford on Avon to see Shakespeare's birthplace and to go inside the original Shakespeare Memorial theatre. In the roof was a big dome like that on St Paul's Cathedral in London and all round the base of the dome was written two famous lines from one of Shakespeare's plays. My father only saw them once, but he could still quote them when I was a boy. That memory served him well at work, as the business was very complex, involving the spare parts of many different sorts of English and imported motorcars. Father could remember all the part numbers for each model and soon became a valuable part of that small business.

Father didn't start in the motor parts business when he left school at the age of 13. There was a bicycle shop a few doors away from his home and that is where he got his first job with the shop owner, Mr Joseph Lucas, who lived over the shop. Dad was his first employee and his job was to clean, repair and service the small acetylene lamps that were used to provide light on bicycles. These lamps worked by having a water compartment at the bottom and a small hole at the top. There was a polished reflector behind this hole. When light was wanted, a small crystal of calcium carbide was dropped into the water through the hole. This reacted with the water and fizzed and a small jet of acetylene gas came up through the hole. This had to be lit with a flint spark or a match and the reflector gave a beam of light, and you pedalled away.

After a year, when he was fourteen, my dad got a better job near the centre of Birmingham with a small business known as J.A. Ryley. They distributed and sold replacement parts for British and imported motorcars. He thought that the motor industry offered a better future than bicycles. This was a new industry. My father's memory was a great asset as they had an ever-increasing stock of motorcar parts and he was invaluable in organising the parts store efficiently. His memory was legendary and sometimes he would be tested by a question such as, "What is the part number for a 1909 Renault 14 crown wheel and pinion?" – and he would tell them. He was always polite, calm and reliable and in due course he became a director. But he did sometimes wonder how life might have been if he had stayed at the cycle shop. Joseph Lucas went on to develop electric lighting for bicycles and all types of vehicles, ships, and aeroplanes and his business became a very successful multi-national company.

My mother, Ada, was born in West Bromwich in

1904. The middle one of five children, she had four brothers. Her father, Albert, worked in a local coal mine until he went into the Army. In 1918, he went to continue the fighting in Ireland. He was shot in the left leg and he could no longer work on the coalface, so he worked as a pony driver, hauling one of the small trucks that took roof supports and other materials to the coalface.

My granddad Albert's father, John, had been a rich man in the local coal mining industry. He had owned three coal mines in the South Staffordshire thick coal seam near to Himley and Dudley Castle. There is a famous house at Himley that is standing on ground that has subsided because the coal underneath had been taken out too close to the surface. The house leans over at about 25 degrees and looks quite alarming. John liked drinking and gambling and on one notable evening he became very drunk and gambled away his three coal mines and was left penniless. That's probably why we referred to him as Uncle John, not Grandfather.

During one of the influenza epidemics, the parents of the family next door to my grandparent's cottage died, leaving five young children, so they took the five children in and they grew up with my mother and her brothers. I only got to know one of those, Frederick. He was always referred to as

Cousin Frederick. He had very poor eyesight and wore the spectacles of that time. They had thick round greenish lenses that made him always recognisable. He looked a bit like an owl.

If we went to visit my mother's parents, we could walk from our home in Repton Road about half a mile to the tramway and get on an electric tram into the town centre. We then changed trams and went to West Bromwich. When we were about halfway there, we were at the town boundary and we had to buy another ticket to the place where Grandmother lived, that was Carters Green. I can remember the boundary as just by the tram stop there was the football ground of West Bromwich Albion, where I sometimes went with my dad if the Birmingham City team were playing West Brom.

To go further and visit Cousin Frederick, we went three more tram stops from Grandma's place so it was quite easy. To get to Grandma's cottage we had to climb 17 brick steps up from the tram stop. There were only two rooms in the cottage: their bedroom and the living room that the front door opened into, and the back door led out to the chickens and the toilet.

In the side wall was a big, black cast-iron range with the fireplace in the middle and the cooking oven on the left and the water boiler on the right. Over the fireplace was a big hook that would hold the kettle and at the front of the fire hole were iron bars close together where you could toast slices of bread on a toasting fork.

Grandma was a tiny person and always happy. She cooked beautiful jam tarts in the fire oven and we ate them fresh and burned our tongues on the hot jam. There were chickens on the bare earth at the back by the earth closet that used to get emptied at night, so occasionally we got fresh boiled eggs.

In the middle of the kitchen Grandma had a big old scrubbed wooden table and sometimes I was given a huge block of salt to play with. I could scrape it with a knife to make a 'sea'. She gave me her two pottery cruets to play with. They were shaped like ships with funnels. One was red and the other was blue and they had two black funnels where the tiny salt and pepper pots fitted. I sailed these ocean liners about in the salt sea for hours. Sometimes I would try to carve the block of salt into the shape of a pig or a dog but it usually fell to pieces.

If we were staying for tea and the weather was fine, Grandpa would take me for a walk. We had two different set walks and each time we were going to go out together he would ask me the same question, "Shall we go up the hill or cross the road?" 'Up the hill' took us about fifty yards up the hill towards the tall clock tower that we could see at Carters Green, then we turned left and walked up Spon Lane until we came to the bridge where the road went over the railway. There was a narrow wooden gate in the wall on our left and going through that gate led us to the long flight of stairs that took us down to the walking space at the side of the rails. We could hear the trucks coming behind us. The rails would begin to vibrate and rattle and we had to stop walking and I stood behind Grandpa, standing quite still until the enormous locomotive came thundering by, making us vibrate as well, completely wrapping us in smoke and steam and leaving us smelling like a coalhouse. All the trucks and carriages rattled by, or were rumbling and slowing if they were going to stop at Swan Village Station, which had facilities for people in those days.

Then it was all quiet and we could see the signals changing and men moving in the signal box and we started to walk along by the rails again until we came to the station. Once or twice, we climbed up the wide wooden staircase that was part of the bridge to walk up and across and down again, to the platform in the other half of the station on the other side of the rails. If we heard bells ringing in the signal box, it usually meant that there was another train coming, so we could go back up onto the bridge and look up and down the lines to see which way it was coming. If we could see it, we would stay there on the bridge and let ourselves disappear in the steam and smoke and when we got home they would say, "You've been playing on that bridge again – you stink!" But it was lovely and frightening and exciting to hold onto the handrail on the bridge and feel it all shaking as if it would explode when the big black engine was right underneath me and shaking all my bones. I had my eyes shut tight and my ears were roaring and bursting and I was out of breath. Then, almost silence. Sometimes in the silence there would be a mysterious smell of soup, as if there might have been a dining carriage or a kitchen going by.

To get away from the railway lines, or train lines, as we called them then, we had to open the small gate for people to get through at the side of the long gates that closed off the road when trains were about to pass. Then we turned left and walked to the main road which had the tram lines in it instead of the train lines and we turned left again to walk up the road until we came to their cottage, 85 Dudley Road, which was completely dwarfed by the gasholder that filled the space between their cottage and the railway station.

Then we came to their wooden gate, which opened outwards over the footpath, as the 17 steps to the cottage door started right from the edge of the footpath. That walk was all climbing up and down lots of steps. We never counted how many, but we were always tired and thirsty when we got home and Grandma's teapot and jam tarts were lovely.

When we chose the walk across the road, we had to start carefully as there were two sets of tram rails set into the road surface for trams coming down the hill from the clock and those coming up the hill heading towards Birmingham. The trams coming down the hill travelled much more quickly than the others and if there was a motorcycle or small car passing the tram between the tram and the side of the road, it couldn't be seen from our side. If it had been raining, the rails set into the road and, level with the road, could be very slippery with dampness and a bit of oil. We would never take a chance and start to cross the road with a tram coming. We just had to stand and wait. As the tram stop was just outside Grandma's gate, we had to move away from the tram stop post, otherwise it looked as if we were waiting to get onto (or 'catch') a tram and we weren't.

Sometimes it took a few minutes to cross. It was a main road and even though there were only a very few private cars, there could be a lot of traffic with lorries and many horse-drawn vans and carts and lots of bicycles threading in and out of the traffic, and people who lived nearby popping out with small shovels and buckets to collect the free fertiliser. Very good for rhubarb; it smelt fresh too.

When we had crossed the road and the tram lines and got safely onto the opposite footpath, we turned left and then right and went along the bumpy lane to the magic attraction – the glassworks.

It was a long, low, stone-built building with wisps of blue smoke coming out of various places in the roofs. There were thick pieces of sooty grey, blue and green glass built into the wall by the road at different heights – for different heights of eyes to peer through. You could see deep red glows in various places and you would just recognise the shady outlines of dark men doing things in front of glowing dark red furnaces, moving and pulling and pushing and shovelling, all indistinctly and a bit like a dark old painting that wasn't very nice. You could feel the heat. The walls were hot on the outside; it must have been hotter inside. What you could see was captivating, even though you couldn't really see it clearly. When we did pull ourselves away from the glassworks, we wandered along the lane, past little old houses where people lived with a bit of land round their place. Pigs were here and there alongside old workshops where people were banging away at their varied trades but couldn't be seen. They were making iron nails and spikes and washers and simple things like that. This walk was so different from the other and the air of modernity and speed and power was missing. The atmosphere wasn't peaceful. There seemed to be lots of activity, but like an anthill there was nothing of the activity to be seen.

Sometimes we went further and got on the tram again and travelled, I think it was three more stops to Great Bridge where Cousin Frederick lived with his two daughters. We three played while the grown-ups talked. Cousin Frederick worked in the local iron-casting factory where they made big iron pipes. He had very poor eyesight and wore those thick, round, green glasses. I don't know if his eyes were naturally weak or if it was because of his work. While we played, sometimes he and Mother talked about their childhood and growing-up time. I heard Mother talk about her life in service and how she was taught to fold the serviettes in three different ways so that they would stand up for breakfast, lunch and dinner. She liked one of the young coachmen but still kept in touch with Charles, now my father, who used to go to see her sometimes when she had half a day off. I know that at one time he thought very seriously about religion and had considered going to Oscott College to train to be a priest. He told me later that he had been much influenced by the work of Cardinal Newman.

I don't know what prompted their decision, but Dad obviously changed his mind about the priesthood and on the day after my mother was 21 they got married and I was born just four years later, at 54 Repton Road, Birmingham, in an ordinary council house in an estate of about a thousand. School was across the road, about 100 yards away.

Chapter 2

Education And The War

I started at Alston Road Infants School when I was five and stayed in the junior school until I was eleven. We had a tarmac playground where all our games were played. I don't remember any grass field that we played on, so I suppose there weren't any football or cricket or athletics or things like that! I had been in the Wolf Cubs and the Scouts and went away to a country camp in the summer. I do remember the names of two teachers. Mr Billings had a white mouse in a glass accommodation arrangement in his classroom and the mouse could be seen going up and down a ladder. The other teacher I remembered was Miss Clay. She had the first class that I was in and we took the secondary school entrance examination during our final year, which determined the school that we went to next. The follow-on schools were more or less academic. The more academic schools were the grammar schools and their quality and curriculum held the possibility of university entrance examinations at age 18. The others didn't.

I passed the grammar school entrance exam and my parents were so pleased that they bought a pair of slippers for Miss Clay. The day for starting at the Saltley Grammar School coincided with the outbreak of World War Two, on 3rd September 1939. As Birmingham was an industrial city, it was considered a likely target for bombing, so we were all sent away, evacuated to a school in the countryside where we might be safer. Some of the teachers had disappeared into the Armed Forces so the education process with two schools of children in buildings designed for one was chaotic, but we did get to play a lot of cricket and sports. Once I scored a hundred runs.

The air raids and bombing took an unpredictable path and the school that we had been sent to was in the countryside but close to an important railway junction, so the area was bombed and we were moved to another school. We went for walks in our local countryside. On one quiet walk, I remembered the day when I was alone on a quiet summer's day. The air was still, the sun was shining in a cloudless sky and I was standing by the hedge, which was intertwined with honeysuckle, and I became aware of a quiet throbbing sound in the air, a bit like a bumblebee. It seemed to get a little louder and I looked up and was quite surprised to see a Junkers 88 bomber German aeroplane flying peacefully towards our town. There were no barrage balloons, no air raid sirens. I could see the black and white crosses painted under the wings and then recognised the throb of the two diesel engines – I think it was the only diesel bomber. It just flew along, minding its own business, and quietly flew away without interference.

Sometimes classes were merged in order to fill the available space. One term I found myself in a class which was in their third year studying classical Greek.

We were placed in houses where the families had children similar in age and gender and in one little house all went well until the husband was killed on the railway. Then his son and I moved to another house with a large family as his mother couldn't cope.

My parent's home was destroyed, so when I did go home in a quiet period of the war, it was to a different house and a different school, but very soon we had a massive air raid. Across the fields we could see Coventry burning and as we were leaving our home to go to the communal air raid shelter, a very large bomb landed just in front of me. My mother, who was about 30 yards in front of me, was projected into the concrete entrance of the air raid shelter and extensively injured. My father, who had just closed the front door of our house, was blasted back against the door and then peppered with shrapnel (jagged pieces of steel from the bomb case) and I saw the blinding flash and deafening roar but felt nothing. I was unharmed while about six houses round me were destroyed and some of my friends were killed.

But at the schools that did have playing fields we had another problem. Due to all manufacturing being focussed on the war effort, there was no cricket equipment being made, so we had no cricket bats or big gloves. But by then the United States had entered the war and there were GIs stationed near to us – and they kindly gave us equipment for playing baseball and trained us as well. I enjoyed it and became a good pitcher and striker.

While the schools were evacuated, and between the ages of 11 and 16, I was sent to six different schools. I was amazed that I learned anything and passed the School Certificate quite well, earning distinctions in maths, chemistry and physics.

The last three stable years at one school had one very useful effect. Although I had had violin lessons when I was younger, I hadn't touched one for years. At the school, George Dixon Grammar School, there were two enthusiastic music teachers. He played the piano, and she was a cellist. With their combined efforts, they formed a school orchestra and a choir.

Birmingham Council had re-established the Birmingham Symphony Orchestra and students could have seats by the great organ for a shilling on Saturday nights. Many of us went.

It was good sitting behind the orchestra as we had a front view of the conductor and could see the soloists very clearly. Two members of the orchestra came to our school each week and gave tuition. One was a trombone player and the other was Mary Chandler, the Principal Oboe. As our school orchestra was short of woodwind players, I was asked to change from violin to oboe, so I did. The music was written similarly so it wasn't too difficult. As a rugby player I had a strong chest which was helpful.

We went to visit other schools to give concerts and developed well. Our climax was when the orchestra and choir were chosen to open the music festival in Birmingham Town Hall. We had an orchestra of 50 and a choir of 80 and performed 'The Heavens are Telling the Glory of the Lord' from Haydn's *Creation*. It went well and was very exciting and has left me with a love of classical music.

As a young boy, I had been in the choir at our local parish church but I had no further interest in religion. It was never mentioned at home as my parents had different views and never went to church.

When I was 16, I went to the local Methodist church as I was rather keen on a girl in the choir and went to classes and was confirmed. My interest waned when I went to university and became more interested in drinking.

In 1946, the war ended and I had been at the school for three years. I passed the university entrance examination and applied for a place at Birmingham University to study Oil Technology and Plastics. But there were new problems. In 1946, I was 18 and conscripted into the RAF where I started my flying training in a Tiger Moth in a sheepskin suit.

The training programme was intensive and had been organised to produce a Spitfire pilot in three months. Losses had been high and the need was great. At the great factory in Bromford Lane – just opposite our Castle Bromwich airfield of 605 squadron – there was one Spitfire produced every day and the traffic on the road was stopped for a few minutes while it was pushed across the road.

The war ended in Europe in 1945 and in the Far

East in 1946 so the Armed Forces recruitment programme was changed. All through the war men had been passing their university entrance examinations, but were taken directly into the fighting forces, so it was decided that, in 1946, they could start coming out and start their university studies. 95% of the university places were reserved for ex-service personnel that year. My flying training was terminated and I was pointed back to university to study coal mining. All places in Oil Technology were full, but there were vacancies in Mining, and I was offered a place on an Honours BSc course, so I accepted it.

Chapter 3

Home And University

As the war had ended, we had the prospect of a real holiday at home, free from high-pressure studies, for a while at least, and we took the opportunity to relax as life steadily progressed to normal again. One of the first things that we did was to remove the air raid shelters that had been dug into the middle of our garden.

On a dreamy day, there was Mother and I pottering in the garden, which had been neglected, and as we were clipping I asked her a question, which seemed to float in from nowhere. "Mother," I said, "Why am I named Edward?"

"I was sure that I was going to have a little girl named Eileen and I had embroidered your sheets and cot pillows and so on with a lovely letter E, so when you were born as a boy, we had to choose a name starting with E and that was the name of the Prince of Wales so we gave it to you. Your middle name, Harry, is your father's middle name too."

I felt rotten and unwanted and said nothing and walked away. One of my friends was a monk who was looking after our parish temporarily as the vicar had moved. He was living on his own in the vicarage and I sometimes went in for a chat. After a few days, I called in to see him. I told him of my rotten feelings and feeling unwanted, then we had a cup of tea. He asked me if I'd heard of 'soul healing'. I said, "No," and he said: "I'll show you." We went into his quiet room and he made it dim. He said, "Close your eyes while I'm praying and then I'll talk to you and ask you to visualise."

I sat quietly in the armchair and almost dozed off. He said, "Ted." I replied: "Yes."

"Keep your eyes closed and visualise another armchair close to yours. Yes. Now visualise a man coming into the room and sitting in the chair. Yes. He's going to talk to you, so listen carefully and when he has finished talking get up and come and tell me his words."

I did and this man in a robe came and sat by me. He said, "Edward." I said: "Yes". He said: "My name is Jesus and I decided that you would be born into this world as a boy."

Silence.

"And I decided that your name would be Edward."

Silence.

"Do you feel happy now?"

"Yes, thank you."

"Goodbye."

Then after a while I stood up and walked over to my friend.

"Very good, thank you."

"Did Jesus come and talk to you?"

"Yes. It was marvellous. Thank you."

During the war, my education had been chaotic due to evacuation to different schools and when I came home, it was to a different home as my parents had been bombed and moved.

By 1945, I came back from evacuation to live at home, which was on the west side of Birmingham and not far from the university so I would be able to travel daily. When I started at the University, the shock was that in that first year in the mining department, which was all male, there were only three of us having come directly from school without any war service experience. The other 17 students were ex-servicemen, having done a lot of active service in tanks, submarines, bombing aircraft and so on. They were tough and their objectives were to work as hard as they could and get well qualified so that they could get as good a job as they could in their new civilian life. Wasting time and larking about was not in their programme. We schoolboys had to work very hard to keep up with them, as did the lecturers, and to deal with their many probing questions. Inevitably their work ethic rubbed off onto us schoolboys and whereas we had been looking forward to the fun and freedom of university life, we found the opposite. Each vacation was not a holiday. We were either working on mountains, studying geological strata, or in caves, and in the long vacations we were sent to work in mines to get practical experience to go with our studies.

I suppose that the effect of this concentrated work ethic was shown in the results that each of us schoolboys achieved. When we started, we felt quite inferior to these war veterans, but at the end of three years we had become quite a close team, with real friendships developed between us. Every evening we talked and debated, worked, and sometimes played bridge together.

After the final third year examinations, the results were due to be displayed at a certain time in the Great Hall of the university. So there we went. I was a bit late, so I was on the outside of the crowd, looking at the noticeboard of the Department of Mining. I worked my way through the crush and peered at the notices. I looked up and down but I couldn't see my name. I felt a big slap on my back and a friend shouted, "Well done Ted!" I said, "I can't see my name," and he pointed to the top of the board where there was a separate section with only two names and one of them was mine. First class honours degree.

I couldn't believe it. Tears ran down my face and I started to squeeze my way away through the noisy crowd. Tears are coming again as I write. The feeling goes all the way back to feeling unwanted and then to the feelings of inferiority that we three schoolboys felt when we started, and now this. I had to get home to share it with Mum and Dad but I knew they'd say well done. I'd leave it at that and probably go to bed until the mountain of emotion subsided. I was sure that their hopes would be satisfied.

Chapter 4

Work

I had applied for a management development position with the National Coal Board and after my application was acknowledged and accepted, I received a note asking me to inform them of my final degree examination results. Now I could do it. In a few weeks I was asked to go for an interview with Mr J. J. Torrence, the general manager of the Leicestershire and South Derbyshire area in the East Midlands division of the National Coal Board (NCB). The East Midlands was the most efficient division of the NCB.

I had a long interview spread over half the morning and half the afternoon just outside Ashby de la Zouch. One of the people that I met was the manager of Donisthorpe Colliery; the mine with the highest output of coal per man shift in the UK.

A few days later, I received a letter offering me an appointment based at Donisthorpe and asking me to go there for another meeting with the manager and group manager. While I was there, I was shown their development plans and their plans to increase productivity even more with the introduction of new machinery from Germany and the United States and I was asked if, besides the normal coalface work, I would keep a detailed record of the progress of these projects. So I found myself some accommodation in the village and started work at Donisthorpe. That was exciting. Even though I had a degree in Mining Engineering, I would have to accumulate five years of varied practical underground work before I could take the examination for the Certificate of Competence as a mine manager.

The introduction of the American machinery was very successful even though we had to train two teams of men to operate the machines, a Dosco Continuous Miner and three shuttle cars. The shuttle cars were battery-driven transporters that had a conveyor along the middle.

One car was positioned behind the Continuous Miner and received the newly-cut coal that poured from the back of the machine. The shuttle car conveyor was moved forwards a bit at a time until the car was full, with about 10 tons of coal. The car had four-wheel drive and four-wheel steering so it was manoeuvred from the workplace to the conveyor that took the coal to the shaft and thence to the surface.

An empty shuttle car replaced the full car behind the Continuous Miner and production continued. We had three shuttle cars so never kept the production machine waiting. With six men, we usually produced about 500 tons of coal a shift, so we soon moved to double shift working and added a 1,000 tons a day to the output of the mine.

While it was exciting to be part of a new team, developing more efficient methods of producing coal and improving the overall performance and the output per man at our mine, Donisthorpe, the process had to be very carefully controlled as we had a highly productive system; that was something that I had to do.

The senior official in charge of that area of the mine had his legal duties to perform as well as overseeing production. He had to patrol all the tunnels and measure the flow of air and test for any signs of those deadly gases, methane and carbon monoxide. He couldn't be in all the vital production places at the same time.

The single part of our production process about which we had to be most careful, was the delivery of the coal that we had produced onto the main conveyor that passed our working area. That big conveyor was carrying the coal from 3 or 4 working places to the shaft and the surface some 3 miles away.

We were producing 500 tons a shift and our shuttle cars carried 10 tons, so there were 50 visits to the main conveyor each shift.

When the shuttle car drivers reached the main conveyor, they had to control the short conveyor in the car and unload the coal onto the main conveyor. This operation had to be done carefully. To let the shuttle car conveyor run and deliver the 10 tons of coal in one big long heap could cause a sudden overload on the main conveyor, which was usually well loaded with coal from the other working faces by then, and that extra 10 tons could cause the main conveyor to stall and stop, then all the other faces loading onto it would have to stop as well and they could all have difficulty in starting again. So it was vital that our shuttle car drivers understood their responsibility. It had to be their own responsibility as I couldn't go backwards and forwards with them to supervise their unloading 50 times a shift.

As they had all been coalface workers themselves, they knew about the problem, but working on the coalface, with the motivation of trying to get your own job done as quickly as possible, didn't necessarily breed the same understanding, or acceptance, of responsibility.

As the main conveyor was about a mile long and carrying about 300 tons of coal, the sudden extra 10 tons of coal could possibly slow it down and even stop it if the electrical power system was also fully loaded, and it could be very difficult to start again so our own discipline was very important. The workman's natural instinct was to unload their car quickly and dash back to the Continuous Miner. We all had to understand the situation and cooperate to keep the whole mine moving. I had to train my men by a mixture of explanation, reminders and discipline.

The consequences of overloading and stalling the main conveyor could be very serious to other coalfaces deeper inside the mine.

I had experienced that myself when working on a conventional pick and shovel coalface, and as an official in charge of one. The problems of being stalled were frustrating. If the coalface conveyor stopped, it was vital that the men working on the coalface ceased shovelling and increasing the load on the conveyor. If our face conveyor became overloaded and then wouldn't start again, it had to be unloaded, and each man had to unload the conveyor in their own place of work which could be

10 yards long. It stands to reason that they weren't going to shovel all the coal back into their working place, having chucked it all out once, so it was shovelled off the conveyor into the waste area behind the conveyor. It was never seen again and a total loss to the mine.

The coalface official was crawling along the coalface which, in some cases, was only 3 feet high, trying to get his conveyor cleared so that it would start again, and then crawling all the way back again and trying to check that his men had got all their roof supports in place while the conveyor was stopped. As the coalface workers were paid by results, they were all frustrated too and frequently gave their supervisor a hard time – this time was extremely stressful.

At these times, tempers became very frayed and I remember one occasion when I was in charge of an area of the mine. I was walking alongside the main conveyor towards the coalface and the official on the face was doing his best and shouting at his men in an angry exchange of bad language – there was never any physical violence as that would have resulted in instant dismissal. When I approached the coalface, he jumped off the coalface with an axe in his hand; he had gone wild in his efforts to restrain his men. He came towards me and laid his head down on the big electric motor that drives the conveyor and pulled off his shirt to expose his neck and said, "Boss, cut my head off, go on, chop it off now. I can't stand it any more."

Yes. Overloaded conveyors that stalled and stopped could cause serious problems that we had to avoid by explanation and control. My men all knew the problems and one of my most effective tools was to threaten to take them out of our team and send them back to work with pick and shovel on the coalface.

The machinery from Germany was used in a completely different way. There was an armoured chain conveyor installed on the full length of a longwall coalface 200 yards long. We had a specially designed coal-cutting machine that rode on the conveyor as if it were a pair of rails. The coal-cutting machine had two cutting blades with chains of tungsten carbide teeth. One blade cut under the coal at floor level and the other blade was bent up so that it cut behind the coal as the cutting machine moved along. Much of the coal fell directly onto the conveyor and one man had a pneumatic pick to break up any large lumps. It was a slower system than the Continuous Miner, but also produced about 500 tons a shift with a higher efficiency of extraction. After 2 years in development work, I had to move into conventional coalface work, doing all the different tasks where were necessary for my qualifications. The excitement of the development work was replaced to some extent when I was moved into the local Mines Rescue Team and trained one day a month at working in fires and floods and a variety of different accidents.

I also continued my studies for the Colliery Manager's Certificate examination. I did this with a recognised correspondence course but found the large amount of work in answering specimen examination questions quite difficult. I was able to take the examination in Stoke on Trent when I was 25 and I was thankful to receive a first class Colliery Manager's Certificate which recognised that I was able to manage any size of mine.

Then I married Jeanette, the daughter of another mine official and we had a son, Mark, born in Burton on Trent and a daughter, Victoria, born in Ashby de la Zouch.

I was then moved to the next mine to gain experience in shaft sinking and tunnelling, where we were using a large amount of explosives. Then I obtained my first management position at Bretby Colliery, as a deputy responsible for a coalface with about 50 men. We bought a small home about 10 minutes' walk from the mine.

My job was quite difficult as I was given the coalface furthest from the shaft to look after. It was a long coalface in a thin seam so it took quite a long time to walk along the tunnels to and from the coalface to inspect them and check the airflow. It also took a long time to crawl all the way through the coalface to inspect each man's work and to check that the roof supports were properly set. Often, if I came to a man having a difficult time, I would stop and help with the shovelling or setting roof supports.

As I gained experience, I was promoted to the position of Overman, and then Afternoon Shift Under-manager at Ellistown Colliery. We had a little coal company owned house just opposite the entry to the mine, and were awakened every morning at 6am by the noise of coal being filled into lorries for delivery.

The mine railway siding went across the end of our little garden and my wife used to get quite upset when the clean washing was covered in bits of soot from the engines. Working in the mine was a hot business and we needed beer to replenish our bodies at the end of each day.

We were both delighted when my next promotion was to Wollaton Colliery in Nottingham as Under-manager and then Manager. My promotion to Nottingham came as a surprise to me, even more so for my wife who had been born in South Derbyshire and always lived there. The villages were mostly similar, with small coal mines and potteries. Many of the local seams of coal have a thick bed of clay underneath them. This is unusual in coal mining as most seams of coal lie on top of a layer of sandstone or limestone, which makes a good hard floor. That was the seabed and the plants that grew there eventually turned into coal.

This clay in Derbyshire and Staffordshire is valuable and usually referred to as fireclay and is used for making pottery. It is usually mined on the same shift as the coal. Fireclay is mined first and sent out on the conveyors. Then the coal is blasted down and loaded off the face. Thus both products are kept clean.

This geological arrangement of coal and fireclay is the reason why the villages are similar, with a small coal mine, a pottery and a brewery or pub. This mixture of production gave people an opportunity to develop a wider range of skills. As well as mining coal, the techniques of working on the potter's wheel and the use of artistic skills and glazing tended to develop better balanced and educated communities.

Working in a pottery kiln, where all the heat for firing the pots came from burning coal, was hard and thirsty work. My wife's mother had worked in the village pottery, where her first job was looking after the men in the kiln. The pottery was well known for its good quality sanitary ware and her first job was to make frequent journeys to the local brewery to fetch a pot full of beer for the men. The pots were freshly made and newly glazed, of course.

Moving to live in a bright light city was going to be an exciting change. Although Nottingham itself had some big coal mines, it had a diverse manufacturing industry; Boots Pharmaceuticals, Player's Cigarettes, Raleigh Bicycles and the famous Nottingham lace.

Whilst we were starting to look at houses and schools, we were also looking round the city with its university, theatres, concert hall and the 100 yards-wide River Trent which had a variety of water sports and sailing.

Then all our exploration ceased as the Middle East war broke out. The Suez Canal was closed and we had no petrol for cars. I couldn't drive the 60-mile round journey to the mine, so temporary accommodation had to be found. My friend, who was a senior official at a neighbouring mine, made enquiries and found a lady on their staff who would have me and her house was about a mile, an easy walk from the mine.

My friend was also friendly with a lady on their staff, so we soon developed a social routine and all played darts and dominoes together in a local pub that had a private room where the landlord and his wife joined us after closing time.

When the Suez crisis was over, I took a week's leave, so as a family we were able to visit the schools and houses and make the plans to move to Nottingham without further delay.

We bought a house in Nottingham near to good schools and enjoyed the pleasures and amenities of living in a clean and civilised place.

The children settled into local schools and my wife learned to drive and began to enjoy life more than she ever had while we were living in mining villages. I had been working at Wollaton for about three years, then one evening I had a surprise. After a Mining Association meeting in Loughborough, I was approached by a mining engineer who had come to the meeting to listen to the speech by the guest speaker, Sir George Dowty. He had been the inventor of the hydraulic landing gear for aircraft. Dowty Mining Equipment Ltd were also important manufacturers of mining equipment.

George Dowty had been an apprentice at Rolls-Royce and later he invented the hydraulic equipment for aircraft. That revolutionised the aircraft industry as it removed the limits on the weight of aircraft now that they could be landed gently.

His company had grown into a large industry and the same hydraulic principles were then applied to roof supports in coal mining, and Dowty Mining Equipment Ltd was employing about 500 people and 'Dowty Pit Props' were used in very many mines.

I was asked if I would like to consider joining their company as they were developing a new range of mechanical mining equipment that would increase productivity and safety. The first coalface to be equipped with this equipment was already operating successfully at a mine nearby, Calverton Colliery, near to Nottingham where we lived.

I looked into the offer and visited Calverton to see the equipment in operation. I decided to leave direct mine management and become an expert in mechanisation.

So I left the National Coal Board and became the Dowty Mining Engineer in the East Midlands. To start with, I concentrated on Calverton Colliery, where the first Roofmaster system was successfully operating. I had to become friends with the management and the operating team of workmen. I worked on that coalface with them to really learn the system. The results were consistently good and the coalface conditions were excellent. The method of working involved a system of total roof caving. The roof behind the coalface was not supported, as on most conventional coalfaces, but it was allowed to collapse as the roof supports were moved forward. Broken stone occupied more space than the former solid roof so eventually the broken stone filled the space left by taking away the coal.

When I started to visit other mines to examine possible new sites for this type of mechanisation, a careful examination of the roof strata was very important.

Eventually the decision was made to install another Roofmaster system at Calverton, where it was known that the geological conditions were right. I worked with the team of miners to install the equipment and stayed with them until all the machines and our Dowty roof support system were working well.

This repeated success at the same mine made a good impression in the whole of the East Midlands division, where there were about 70 coal mines. From then on, my own selling efforts had to extend, and with the co-operation of the Calverton team, we were able to show these operating systems to many interested mining engineers from the UK and countries abroad – the USA had the greatest potential. In the next 5 years we installed 10 Roofmaster systems locally with a value (then) of about a million pounds.

After success in the UK, I helped in developing the export markets and, after a long time working abroad, I came home to find that my wife, Jeanette, had a replacement for me so a whole series of changes took place and I found myself in the role of Senior Lecturer in Marketing. To sharpen my skills, I took a degree course at Warwick University and got a Masters degree in Marketing, specialising in the international field.

As part of my duties, I had to lecture in Cheltenham once a week. In the morning I was at a boy's school and the class was mainly 17 year olds. They were studying Commercial Art and Design. They each had their independent projects to work on so I made brief notes and asked them to continue. In time for our meeting next week, I would prepare notes related to the market for their projects, which we would discuss individually.

In the afternoon, I moved to a different school where the students were of a similar age, but they were all young ladies who had been studying Fine Art and were now considering Commercial Art, so they were examining their work from a different point of view. After our introduction, their class tutor was away until the end of the afternoon, so I was examining their work.

When the class tutor came back, it was time for

them to leave, so she invited me to the staffroom where we would have a cup of tea and discuss the teaching situation. There was no-one else in the room so she made a tray of tea and we sat at a pair of large armchairs with a table in between. She had short curly black hair and wore dark horn rimmed spectacles. When she removed them, her face she looked much more attractive. She asked if I played rugby or football. I told her of my background in the coal mining industry and of some games at university and for Birmingham and she said that she could see that I was quite muscular. I drank some tea and she asked when it would be a convenient time to discuss the Marketing teaching programme. Obviously, it wasn't now as I had a long drive back to Hertfordshire.

She suggested that if I stayed the following Tuesday evening, that would allow time for a discussion. Her flat wasn't far away and she would arrange for some supper.

I thanked her and said that would be fine, but I would leave now and drive back to Hertfordshire. She walked to the car with me and said goodnight with a very light kiss.

The next Tuesday morning, my car was hit head-on by a car that came out to overtake a lorry travelling in the opposite direction to me. The front of my car was smashed in, I was trapped and covered in broken glass and I had a broken neck. I think that my hearing had been damaged during the tunnelling work that I had done as we didn't have protection from the effects of the explosives. The need for help with hearing only became apparent when I started teaching in the academic environment.

In the Royal Hospital in Cheltenham, the X-rays showed two broken vertebrae and three smashed discs. When I moved my neck, there was a nasty grating feeling, but at least it did move. After I recovered and started back to work, driving was difficult as I had to wear a big support collar. Each time I turned my head there was pain in my neck and a very sickly grinding feeling. If I used my hearing aids, the grinding noise was very loud, with this unpleasant sensation of bone on bone in my neck. I think that my hearing was probably damaged for the first time when I went to Rawdon Colliery (next to Donsithorpe) for tunnelling and blasting experience.

I married again and we lived in a delightful small Elizabethan House in a very quiet village on a country estate. But then work started to build the M25 London circular motorway. To avoid some of the roadworks and congestion, the lane through our village became a very busy shortcut and life became difficult and dangerous for people living there.

At that time too, my wife had been having treatment for a heart condition and she had been advised, if it ever became possible, to live somewhere warmer and quieter. So we decided to look around. One week we hired a motor caravan for a week and explored the south coast of Cornwall where we had family and friends. We both had an interest in growing grapes and making wine as a hobby. We didn't find anywhere suitable, but after we had returned home, my son saw a place in a local paper and sent us the details. It looked good, so we went to Cornwall for the weekend and decided to buy the place. It was an old dairy farm with 50 acres, with some cider apples already growing there. We planned to create a vineyard and cider apple orchards and to produce wine and cider on the farm to sell from our own shop. I also started to develop a range of Cornish liqueurs, starting with a sloe liqueur as we had plenty of sloes growing there. We were busy in the business and in the local choirs and amateur dramatic societies where Gilbert and Sullivan productions were popular. We enjoyed our own products too and I think our own social consumption of alcohol got higher. I was working and coping with the pain in my neck with a combination of painkillers, careful posture and a certain amount of alcohol. I couldn't continue with my hobby of wood carving as the impact of the mallet on the chisel made me squeal and shudder. We used to enjoy the choral singing in the churches, particularly near to Christmas time when the delightful and original Cornish carols were sung. In some of the old traditional Methodist churches, the congregation knew the hymns and sang the four-part harmony, which we really enjoyed singing too.

One Sunday evening I decided to go to a big service in the Chapel Street Methodist church in Penzance which was really old and had a balcony and held about 1,500 people. It was the climax of a missionary day and there would be plenty of good singing.

I got there about seven o'clock and the service was due to start at 7.30pm. As usual, there was a group of young musicians playing well-known hymns and some people sang with them and others just chatted between themselves. I didn't see anyone there that I knew; we lived about 24 miles away.

As it was a special service, hymn sheets with about 20 well-known hymns on them had been given out and some people were singing these hymns. Then the service began and the visiting preacher, who was a missionary, climbed up the steps into the old-fashioned pulpit that was level with the balcony. The preacher was obviously a jovial man and began by saying, "Good evening. I've been listening to the music and to your singing and it seems to me that you enjoy singing hymns. Is that correct?" Many people responded with a loud "YES." So then he said: "That is good. Let us begin our service by singing the first six hymns on the hymn sheet." So the music started and we sang. That was just like a storm of sound that went on and on. He conducted us and sang with us full of enthusiasm until we finished number six. Then we all flopped into our seats.

The service went on. During the singing of one of the hymns later, I noticed an odd feeling. Something was going on inside my neck; a sort of twisting sensation. If you have ever seen a thick rope being made, you will have seen that it is made by twisting a bunch of thinner ropes together. These ropes are twisted in the opposite direction to the parts of the inner rope. If you twist it one way, the ropes will get tighter. If you do it the opposite way, the ropes will get looser. It was that sort of twisting and untwisting motion that seemed to be going on in my neck. It lasted about half a minute, then stopped.

I kept on singing and then sat down, mystified.

I was on my way home from Penzance when I realised that I had no pain in my neck. I was very unsure about that and I didn't tell anyone about it. A few days later I had to go and see my doctor as he was concerned about my chest. I had been a heavy smoker. After more examinations, he decided to send me to Penzance Hospital for a chest X-ray. I asked him if they could X-ray my neck at the same time. He knew that it had been broken in the car accident and I had asked him previously about possible treatment. I made the appointment with the hospital the following day and went for the X-rays to be taken. They would be delivered to the doctor a few days later. Then I received a call from the doctor's office, asking me to go and see him. I did and he said that my chest was OK and didn't need treatment. I asked about my neck and he looked at the pictures and said he didn't think it was my neck. They may have sent the wrong pictures. He said that he would contact the hospital and contact me again. When he did, he said that we seem to have a mystery as these pictures showed no damage to my neck at all. He would contact me again. I still didn't tell him about that twisting sensation, but I knew then that my neck had been healed. I've just rolled my head into all sorts of positions and there is still no problem or no pain and the movement is normal. I stopped taking the painkillers.

During that service in the Methodist church in Penzance, my neck had been healed. No-one there knew me. There had been no prayers for me, no laying on of hands. Nothing. I am eternally grateful that I have been healed. I had told no-one except my wife at the time, Maria, but she wasn't particularly interested in my personal welfare or church or spiritual matters.

Life carried on normally – the business was successful and our consumption of alcohol increased. On a fine evening I would take our Staffordshire bull terrier, Emma, for a walk down to the beach where she could run about. After sitting in the evening sun and chatting to whoever was there, we would go into the Five Pilchards where I had two pints of Cornish bitter and Emma lay across my feet in a proprietorial manner.

Then we went home. It was a slower journey uphill with beer. It was always easy to restrict my consumption of beer to two pints as I knew that there was plenty more booze at home. In later years, when I had been cured and didn't drink alcohol at all, I heard people say that they'd never seen me drunk. I knew that I had to maintain that sober image. I had an alcohol business to run. I was a respected member of the church. I had to serve my customers and drive my delivery van, so I kept up that sober image. Later in the day, when we were safe in the house, we enjoyed our drinking and when my wife had gone to bed I drank more and more.

My life became a simple routine: farm work, church, and the pub, plus the amateur theatre. When we were doing a show, I often took a small bottle of brandy on the stage with me and then I didn't have any stage fright. Maria used to spend her time walking in the woods, on the beach and visiting various friends, which included some flights from Newquay to London where her daughter was married to a consultant and they had two lovely children. They all used to come and stay with us at times and brought their smart boat.

As the drinking increased, we grew further apart and slept in separate rooms and my behaviour got worse. One night I staggered up to bed and when I went into my room the light bulb flickered and went out. I remember thinking that I would fit a new one in the morning and I went to sleep.

I was awakened by a click, but the light didn't come on. I turned over to look at the doorway. I could see Maria outlined against the light at the top of the stairs. She was leaning towards me and I started to roll away. A kettle of boiling water was poured over my shoulder and the kettle thrown at me. As I screamed, she fled. I heard her clatter down the stairs. I heard the bang of the heavy front door closing. I heard a car start and squeal away up the gravel drive. She and Emma were gone.

I lay there in pain, all wet and paralysed and trying to think through my alcoholic haze. It was half past one. I stretched out slowly and reached for the phone. I knew which button to press for Anthony next door. The phone rang for a long time and then a tired voice answered. It was Anthony. I mumbled my story to him and he said: "Don't move. I'm coming." I thought, *At least she missed my face.*

In about 10 minutes, I heard his old Land Rover arrive and he came up the stairs with a big torch and a spare overcoat. He wrapped me up and found my shoes and got me down the stairs. I gave him the house keys and he took me to the emergency department at Penzance Hospital. They got me into bed and treated me and told Anthony that I'd be there for a few days. When the scalds were responding to treatment, they rang Anthony and he came and took me home. Anthony's brother was Roger. Roger's wife Karen was my cousin and she had been in our home and tidied up and got rid of a lot of empty bottles. They told my doctor that I was at home and his wife, who was the district nurse, came to dress my scalded arm and shoulder every day. Karen brought me a cooked meal every evening and I had more visits from our church people than I had had in years. I only had an occasional glass of wine plus quite a lot of medication. Then either

Anthony or Roger came in for a chat each evening, and saw me properly into bed. It was winter so the shop was closed and there was not much work to do on the farm.

When I was quite a lot better and able to drive my van again, I started to shop for myself and started socialising again. I took the opportunity of having no planned time to travel and see more of Cornwall. I was able to visit a few other Christian spiritualist churches, and I even treated myself to a day on the Isle of Scilly. I loved that old boat, *The Scillonian*, and especially enjoyed settling in a sunny corner on deck, sheltered from the breeze and reading one of the big newspapers.

When I was in places well away from home, I did hear mentions of someone who sounded like my wife. If I could find her, I knew that I might be taking a risk in going to see her, but if I could find her I'd like her to see that I wasn't drunk. But then I never used to be in the daytime.

Somehow I found where she was living. It was quite an out-of-the-way place and I parked where she would be able to see my van and I walked apprehensively up her path. Her car was there. When I knocked on the door, I heard a furious barking which I recognised and then the door opened a little. I could hardly see her face. She spoke harshly, "What do you want?"

"I don't really want anything except to know where you are and how you are and to tell you that I'm not angry with you."

She said: "I'm alright."

"May I come again?"

"I suppose so."

I walked away without looking back. I thought, *That's strange, I didn't hear Emma barking anymore.* Perhaps she recognised my voice.

I was pleased that I knew where Maria was and that I had been brave enough to go and see her, but for now that was enough. At a spiritualist church near to Penzance, I was sitting down after the service, having a cup of tea with one of the mediums, and she asked me if I ever saw my former wife. I said that I had seen her once and she was probably starting divorce proceedings and that was probably the best way for things to go. The medium said that she thought that I should go to see her again. I did say that I hadn't any reason to, but she said, "Just go." We left the matter there after she said that she didn't know the person at all.

The following week I was visiting my cousin Robert, who lives at Hayle, and as I left I thought that as I was close to where Maria was living, I would try and call and see her again. So I did and parked in the same place so that she could see my van.

The routine was the same as my previous visit but this time the door opened wide and she invited me in and offered me a cup of tea. She said that she was glad that I had come as she had a problem with the top of the stairs, which were very old, and she knew that I did a lot of building work so I could advise her.

After the tea, we went up the stairs, which were narrow, and led directly into the only room upstairs, which was now her bedroom. The sun had come out and the room was getting hot, so she opened the window wide. She showed me the top of the stairs and I poked into the stair wood and found it to be going rotten and beginning to come loose in the wall. No more could be seen as the wall was plastered.

I got up and started to talk to her and to explain what the problem appeared to be, but I could see that she wasn't listening to me. She seemed to be vacant and her eyes had a faraway staring look. She began to tremble and shake and sob, and as I moved forward to try and comfort her, she screamed at me and swore at me with all sorts of foul language and hatred, telling me to go away, go away, go away, and put her hands over her ears so that she couldn't hear me.

It was horrible and frightening, but I knew from my experience of dangerous situations underground that I was in no physical danger and that nothing would harm me.

I stood still and said a prayer to Jesus and Mary and the Holy Spirit and I felt strong. She was still shouting and swearing and I moved towards her, shouting out the name of Jesus and making a big sign of the cross with my arms. Somehow I knew that she was possessed by a devil and I shouted to the devil:

"Devil be gone in the name of Jesus.

Devil come out of her and go away."

I kept making the sign of the cross and walking round her as she shook and screamed incoherently. I kept making the sign of the cross and approached her, right up to her face, still repeating the name of Jesus in a strong voice. With my fingers I made the sign of the cross on her forehead and shouted again, "Devil be gone!"

A change started to happen, there was a swelling on her left shoulder and something began to emerge. It was a dark green jelly sort of thing about two feet high and something like the shape of a monkey. It quivered and then it jumped across the room onto the frame of the window that was open. Then it jumped down onto the grass and sort of hopped down the path to my van and then it turned right and disappeared towards the road.

She was lying on the bed, exhausted and almost asleep. I didn't know what to do but I knew that I must leave her still and not wake her up after what had happened.

I really didn't know what to do but I did know how to get in touch with a senior person in one of the local spiritualist churches, so I phoned her and explained what had been going on. She said that she would contact a lady who was one of their church members and lived nearby. She would be asked to come and meet me and hear all about the situation and stay until Maria woke. Then she would stay with her until I left and if necessary get someone else to help. When she came, we were able to contact a local doctor and ensure that they knew the situation, and got the district nurse to visit to see if help was needed. I didn't know what to do but now that I have written this I will seek our local vicar to ask if there is any recognised routine process to be followed in cases of possession.

I moved the top of her dress so that I could see her shoulder and there was no mark or cut or red place in her skin or any sign of where it had come out of her body.

Later the lady came and all was explained, and when Maria woke it was all explained to her. After more cups of tea I came home. Now I feel drained as well from writing all this and pulling out these memories, so I need to put down my pen and be quiet.

I did and I slept for an hour and I feel a little better now but I'm still shaken by that frightening experience. Now I have put on a rosary made from wooden beads and with a wooden cross. Sheila taught me how to make simple rosaries a long time ago as she is an expert, and it really is surprising how wearing a rosary really makes a difference to how I feel. I certainly feel safer. I have seen Maria again and we did not discuss what happened during my visit. I don't think we will meet again as she will be proceeding with divorce arrangements, because of my bad behaviour related to drinking, and now we live a long way apart across the sea.

While Anthony was helping me recover, we talked about many things, including the mains water supply to the farms. He said that it wasn't satisfactory for keeping equipment clean so he had had a borehole put in to provide his own clean drinking water supply. Our water from the taps in the farmhouse was sometimes brown and frequently came out with a lot of bubbles in a milky white colour.

I asked him what I had to do to get a borehole and a clean water supply, and he told me about a visit from a dowser and if I wished he would contact the man and ask him to come. He came and brought his wife, who also dowsed, and after establishing how much water we needed, they set off walking round the farm. When they came back, they reported that there were two places where a borehole would produce what we needed. They also said that there were a lot of underground streams on the property. That fitted in with the original name of the farm in the Cornish language; Parc an Tidno, meaning Farm with Springs. You can't find the word *tidno* in a Cornish dictionary. The Cornish word for spring is *fenton* and the plural is *fentonau*, which is shortened in common usage to *tidno*. We chose a convenient site and the dowser said that he would arrange for his son to come and do the work as it was his son who operated the tractor and drilling equipment. I asked: "What if that amount of water didn't come?" He replied: "Then you don't pay us anything."

The whole operation was successful and he found an excellent water supply. The borehole was 150 feet deep, below sea level.

The skin on my arm, shoulder, and back was now all healed so the daily visits of the nurse ceased and I returned to solitary loneliness. My drinking continued as before, but without the company of my dog. I just got worse and worse and went to bed with a bottle of whisky either side of my bed so that when I woke in the night I could easily find my comforter. I was in such a state that when I did get up, I just wandered round the farm and I didn't know what to do. I grew a big beard out of laziness. I think the village postman kept the local people informed on how I was.

One day, some friends from the village came to see me and told me that there was to be a healing service at a local church and told me to be ready at 6pm as they were going to take me. Anyone could have taken me anywhere. I was like a donkey.

They came and fetched me and took me to the service, which was at Trelowarren Chapel. I went in with them and sat with them but I did nothing. I just sat there all the time. No singing, no standing up, no prayers, nothing. So they brought me home again afterwards. Later in the next week, they came to visit me again and told me that there was another healing service and it would be a complete healing weekend with lots of people taking part. They came and fetched me again and took me to Trelowarren again and I went in with them again and sat there like a lump of rock all through the service and the healing procedures afterwards. I sat there all the time and stayed there until the church was empty. Then I stood up and shuffled up to the front of the church where a big rough wooden cross was put up for the healing service.

I went up to the cross and put my arms round it and hung onto it and I said: "I forgive my wife Maria for injuring me with the boiling water." I didn't know where the words came from or why. It wasn't me speaking consciously, but that is what I said.

Then I turned round and walked out of the church into the common room where they were having tea. My friends were by the door and saw me.

"Hello Ted. You do look better."

"I am better."

"Would you like a cup of tea?"

"Yes please."

I was actually speaking normally.

I had my tea and we talked a bit, then went back to our village. We sang hymns all the way and I joined in. They saw me into the house and said: "We'll see you tomorrow."

"Yes, OK. You will be welcome."

In the morning they came and I made tea and we talked and then walked and I went home with two of them for lunch and then walked home and went to bed.

I've never had another drink of alcohol since that day. Since that moment of forgiveness, I have never drunk another drop of alcohol in my life. I am completely healed of the addiction to alcoholism, but I knew that my brain was damaged and I couldn't think logically and I was still shy and felt like a mouse when in the company of others, men or women. I did need to feel like John Wayne again. I was sober, but there was a gap in my feeling and emotions.

Another friend from the village came to see me and asked if we could sit down and talk about alcohol. I said I didn't want to talk about alcohol; I wanted to forget it. He explained to me that alcoholism is an addictive illness recognised as such by the World Health Organisation and he went on to tell me about the affects that ethyl alcohol has on various parts of our body. Our liver and kidneys have to deal with it and can become destroyed. Our brain and memory can be seriously affected and it can be up to five years after stopping drinking before they might begin to function normally again. They may never recover. Our emotions are twisted up and we have usually damaged our relationships with other people while we have been drinking and our own self-esteem can be rock bottom. Once the anaesthetising effect has gone away, we are more aware of our feelings and what people think about us. We will usually start to remember many of the bad things that we were doing – stealing in order to get alcohol, hurting by being rude to people, being aggressive and often having feelings of remorse and worthlessness even though we aren't drinking anymore.

He asked me if I knew anything about an organisation called Alcoholics Anonymous; that was started by drunks to help each other. I didn't. He told me how helpful it had been to him and, unlike most self-help organisations, it welcomed new members who were drunks and there were no charges or fees to pay.

I realised that I had been drinking alcohol for about forty years so it was likely that some parts of me were affected. I knew that my memory was hopeless and I didn't care too much about missing birthdays or giving presents, so my close family relationships were poor.

I began to get stronger. Each day I tried to walk round a different field on the farm to really catch up with what the situation really was, although I didn't expect to stay there much longer, with the prospect of divorce getting closer. Eventually I checked the little yellow tractor all over for oil and grease and battery and diesel and I started it and started to mow in between the vines in the vineyard, which really did look a mess. As I was coming towards the end of one row of vines, I saw a big badger shuffling along in the space at the end of the rows. I stopped the engine and just sat there silently. The badger came up to the tractor, sniffed at it and slowly walked all round it, then continued on his way past the end of the rows. He took no notice of me and it felt lovely being so close to a wild animal that wasn't frightened of me at all! I had never been as close to a badger before. I sat there quite a while before I started mowing again. There were 40 rows of vines, each about a quarter of a mile long, so that was about 10 miles to mow, going along each row twice in the opposite direction. That was about 40 miles to mow in bottom gear, leaning over and pruning the tops of some of the vines as I passed them. That took a week if the weather was fine. Anyone that came to the farm could tell where I was as the tractor had an air-cooled diesel engine and that was noisy, but it was economical.

The legal process of the divorce dragged on and I wasn't very interested. I would have no work and nowhere to live but it didn't seem to matter and I plodded on. I was 65 now and getting a bit of pension money. The farm had been valued at £180,000 and Maria was to get half when it was sold.

One day, a smartly dressed man drove into the farmyard and, after some confused conversation about the change of address and the Cornish names, he told me that he was looking for Mr Edward

Jeffries. That was myself, and I had to go and find something that was acceptable as proof of identity and then he introduced himself and gave me his card. We went into the old farmhouse to sit down.

He then explained to me that the insurance company that he worked for had taken over another small company some years ago. The small one was the University Life Assurance Company with which I had taken out a small policy when I was 21. I had forgotten about that completely and the payments were small enough not to be noticed in my bank statements, which had been quite complicated. He prepared paperwork for me to sign and I had to give my current bank details and he said that when it had all been checked in the main office they would be paying about £65,000 into my bank account. I was amazed.

The next day I went to see my farm insurance company, NFU, and they agreed to make me a loan of £30,000 secured on the farm. That meant that I could pay the divorce settlement and remain living on the farm and continue to develop the business. It seemed like another miracle, as I had lost all hope. It was getting close to Christmas.

One day the phone rang and a very quiet lady's voice introduced herself and explained that she had met some other dowsers and one of them had told her that he had visited the farm, looking for a source of water for a borehole. He said that while he and his wife had been exploring the farmyard, they had identified some very interesting and strong fields of energy and as she was interested in these things herself could she come and explore them by dowsing for herself? I said of course she could and a date was arranged. She arrived and introduced herself as Sheila.

She spent a whole afternoon there and sometimes I saw her sitting quietly as if she was asleep. She came to the farmhouse when she had finished and we had a cup of tea. I asked her a few questions and she was hesitant with her replies, and said that sometimes it was difficult explaining energies to people as it could conflict with their own beliefs. She had found some very interesting energy patterns and thought that there had been people living there for a very long time. She told me that she was a teacher of infants and had trained in art. She lived near the top of a well-known hill, so a few weeks later, when I was passing that way, I called at the place where she lived and I saw her there with a variety of animals.

There were holes kicked in all the panels in the sides of the caravan that she lived in and much of the inside was smashed. She was painting a lovely emotive picture of flowers. I told her that I had a couple of empty barns on the farm and she would be very welcome to use one of these as a studio if she thought it would be suitable as there were no animals at Porthallow Vineyard now.

That's how we met, and eventually she came to live at the farm. That was the beginning of the happiest ten years of my life. I realised that if I had still been drinking, Sheila wouldn't have had anything to do with me.

Alcohol had been a big factor in the breaking up of her previous marriage too. Later on we discussed marriage but recognised that we had both had very painful experiences and didn't want to do it again. Our relationship was lovely and she soon made lots of friends nearby. She wasn't far from all those that she had moved away from and often had meetings with them when she taught meditation and other spiritual matters. I didn't get involved.

Chapter 5

Tractor Accident

I was using two tractors regularly at the vineyard. The small yellow one, the Leyland, was chosen to fit between the rows of vines for moving and spraying. The big green one was more powerful and was best for cutting down the grass and weeds in the fields where we had planted trees in place of the cows. There were about 35 acres of trees to look after, but as they had all been planted two metres apart in a rectangular pattern, mowing between the rows was easy.

On this fine day at the vineyard, I decided to spend a few hours cutting the grass in Spring Meadow. We often walked along the path to the meadow together in the evening. It was overhung with trees and very peaceful. We always stopped at the first gate where we could lean against the wall and be out of the way. Solomon, our cat, always came with us and shot up a tree and out onto a branch where he could see everything. I think he was at home with the elves and the fairies there.

We stopped at that gate as it was opposite to the big slope at the edge of Bank Field, where there were many badgers living in their setts under the big tree roots. We used to rest there quietly and sometimes a badger would come along the lane, slowly sniffling at anything he found. We stood quite still and silent and the badger would often stop when he came to our boots. He would explore all round them but never looked up. Then, when he seemed satisfied that all was well, he would continue on his way. These were magical moments and we felt very privileged to share them. The meadow had been an acre of absolute wilderness. It had been so densely overgrown that even the bullocks never tried to get in there.

When we were drawn to clean it out, we found a beautiful winding stream coming from an unusual circular spring. It was like a glass bowl, about two feet across, with the water bubbling up through a hole in the middle.

It was very close to some grassy hummocks at the side of the field, which were surrounded by a stone wall about four feet high. Nowadays, a Cornish hedge is the normal boundary and is made from two dry stone walls with soil in the gap between. When this little area was dowsed later, the consensus was that these had probably been human dwellings in the Iron Age period. Choosing to live close to a spring of pure drinking water would be logical. The site was about 10 minutes' walk from the sea but hidden from view by the hills that formed the top of the cliffs.

I had built a wooden bridge across the stream so that I could cross it with a tractor to mow both sides of the field. Spring Meadow had a lovely ambience and it was one of our favourite places for a picnic. We would stretch out our legs and lean back onto the walls that were covered in wildflowers, including orchids.

I mowed the middle part of the field and then started to mow more slowly round the edges to make it tidy. I was mowing close to the wall on the left-hand side. In that direction, the mower delivered its cuttings at the foot of the wall and we could sit on clean grass. The tractor was in the lowest gear and with its four-wheel drive had a powerful pull. I was concentrating on the steering, because if I kept the front wheels about four inches from the wall, the mower would be very close to it and leave it tidy.

I was not looking up at the branches of the trees

and I heard an almighty CRACK, a frightening bang and then a thick branch crashed down just in front of my face. It smashed the tractor's vertical exhaust pipe and the steering wheel that I was holding and came to rest, denting the dashboard, the engine cover, and the steel covers at the sides of the tractor.

Instinctively my left foot had pushed down the clutch so the tractor had stopped moving forwards and I was able to reach the control that stopped the engine.

When I collected my wits, I was able to reach the gearbox and put the gears into neutral. My hands were free, but I was trapped into the tractor as the branch, which was about six inches thick, had come to rest across my knees and thighs with the smashed steering wheel underneath.

The amazing thing was that the branch had crashed down, smashing the steering wheel, but as I was driving the tractor both hands were on the steering wheel. The branch had passed straight through my wrists and hands before breaking the steering wheel down into pieces. My hands were untouched, undamaged, and now resting on top of the branch.

I was isolated about half a mile from the farmhouse – I couldn't blow the horn as the controls were all smashed and I couldn't get off the tractor as my legs were completely trapped in by this branch. I was resigned to staying there and waiting.

When I looked around, I could see what had happened. The branch had been sticking out over the field but I had been looking down at the front wheels of the tractor to try and keep them about four inches from the field wall. The safety frame on the tractor, which was behind my seat, had caught the branch and started to pull it. As the tractor was in bottom gear and also in four-wheel drive, to mow slowly and precisely it had maximum pulling power and kept pulling the branch until something had to give way.

The branch was solid and about six inches thick so it hadn't broken away from the tree. I could see that the end of the branch was still attached to the tree trunk, but the tree was dead and had been rotting away inside. The whole of the inside of trunk was gone, leaving about an inch thickness of wood all round. As the pulling power of the frame on the tractor had reached the limit of the old tree's strength, it had suddenly broken off a complete ring of the dead trunk. It was elm and very hard wood.

The loud crack was the tree breaking just before it fell onto me and the tractor.

My thighs were painful where the branch had landed on them, but there was no pain in my hands or arms at all, yet the branch had crashed through them. No bits of me were broken. The branch had just passed through my arms as if they were shadows.

I was amazed and I just sat still, trying to understand. I couldn't and I couldn't attract attention. It was a pleasant morning and I decided to stay quiet and try to be grateful.

Eventually Sheila had noticed the silence in the fields and came to look round. She walked along the path to Spring Meadow and saw me on the stationery tractor.

She came over to me, saying, "What on earth have you been up to?"

She surveyed the scene and tried to understand what had happened. She could see that I couldn't get off the tractor and we agreed that the best thing would be to try and get Anthony or Roger to come round in one of their big tractors and bring one of my chainsaws from the farmyard.

So Sheila went and then came back to tell me that Anthony would come in about half an hour, and she brought a flask of tea. I enjoyed a cup and she went back to the farmyard to wait for him. I could hear his tractor coming from about a mile away. Our farms are on opposite slopes of the valley. If the air is still, you can even hear conversations in the other farmyard. Anthony drove into the meadow – I could see his son Simon as well with a chainsaw. Sheila was walking behind.

The big tractor came safely over my wooden bridge and stopped. The men got down and came to look at me. They didn't really know what to say as it was obvious what had happened. The broken tree trunk, the big branch, and me. They tried to lift the branch by themselves but it was too heavy.

Anthony asked, "How did you get your hands out, Ted?" I had to say that I hadn't got them out, they just were out. I couldn't explain what had happened. It just had.

They thought it best to cut the branch in two places – just by the trunk piece and at the other end of the tractor. They were then able to lift the branch off the tractor and off my legs. It was about six feet long. I got off the tractor very gently and we drank the tea.

Anthony and Simon looked at the damage on my tractor and where the seat was. It was just in front of the safety frame. There were three big dents on either side where the branch had crashed onto the mudguards and in the middle where it had landed on the gearbox after smashing the steering wheel. There were just the two spaces either side of the gearbox, where my legs had been, with the broken steering wheel on top of the gearbox.

Anthony said: "It looks like a job for Roger Kueck." (pronounced Cook). Roger lived just opposite their farm. He had a small farm growing mainly cauliflowers and early potatoes but also had two large buildings where he serviced and repaired tractors and manufactured cauliflower harvesting machines.

Roger's father had been a German prisoner of war who worked on farms in Cornwall and decided to stay when the war ended. Roger was always friendly and helpful and did his repair jobs in the most practical and economical way. One day I had taken my yellow tractor up to him as sometimes the exhaust smoke was black as if it was burning oil. He said that the piston rings were probably worn. I asked if it could be fixed and he said, "Yes, but we'll have to take the cylinder head and the sump off to do it."

I asked what it might cost and he said, "About £200. But how long have you had it?"

"About 20 years."

"Well it isn't going to get any worse. How much oil do you have to put in?"

I said about a gallon a year.

So he said, "That's costing you about £5 so I should leave it alone." He was honest.

That was 10 years ago and the tractor is still running well.

So as they were here and had a big chain with them, they offered to tow my tractor to Roger Kueck's place on their way home. Anthony said again: "How did you get your hands out?" He looked at my red denim shirt and it wasn't scratched or torn, the cuffs were still buttoned and there wasn't a tear anywhere.

I had to say rather sheepishly, "I just don't know what happened. The branch seems to have gone straight through my hands as they were holding the steering wheel. Perhaps it was a miracle." Silence followed.

I helped them put their chain under the front of the tractor and they lifted its front wheels off the ground and drove round the field and over the bridge and away.

Sheila and I walked back to the farmhouse, with Solomon. We needed a rest and sat by the fire while our thoughts settled. I was full of gratitude at not being physically hurt. We both felt rather overwhelmed that we may have experienced another miracle.

Chapter 6

Landscape Zodiacs

Landscape Zodiacs are arrangements of various features of the landscape to form figures shaped like the signs of the astronomical zodiac. The word 'zodiac' is derived from the Greek *zoös*, life. The signs have been identified by looking at the stars in the sky and identifying patterns similar to objects that we know on the ground.

The most well-known shape in the sky is probably the Plough, a group of stars near to Polaris, the North Pole star, used for navigation.

This star is easily found on a clear night by looking at the north sky and picking out the group of stars that are like a plough with a long handle. The handle points to Polaris.

There are many other figures that can be imagined to be like living creatures. They have been known for thousands of years and may have Arabic or Latin names. They include Leo, the lion, Taurus, the bull, Cygnus, the swan, etc.

For reasons that we do not know, similar figures were made on the surface of the Earth thousands of years ago. These are known as Landscape Zodiac figures. They often incorporate natural features such as hills and ponds and use large stones, megaliths, to mark significant features such as the ends of the swan's wings.

There is a well-known zodiac on the land in Somerset and Sheila was born in a village which is inside the figure of the lion, so she has always been aware of zodiacs. We put her practical experience, together with my knowledge of astronomy, when she discovered the lion in Cornwall. Then we identified the complete set of figures, some of them miles across. These are described in detail in her book *Cornwall's Landscape Zodiac* which is available from Amazon, or signed copies are available from her website.

We worked happily together in the landscape, pursuing the knowledge of Landscape Zodiacs that she had had for years.

Great stones (megaliths) are found in groups in many countries, stretching from Britain through North Africa and Egypt and as far as Persia. In detailed surveys of these arrangements of stones, it has been established that many of the sites have alignments pointing to rising and setting points of the sun and certain of the brightest stars.

During the period from 2000 to 1500BC, when these stones were erected in Britain, only a few of these great stars actually rose above the horizon, or set, so when the alignment points directly to those rising and setting places on the horizon, we can be sure that the stones were used for timekeeping at night.

In Egypt and other countries, there were many ancient writings about the stars so we know that they were an important aspect of life to mankind. In Britain we have no such written records, but research by Sheila Jeffries has revealed fascinating facts about the relationship between the megaliths and the stars on *The Lizard Peninsula* in Cornwall, where she lived.

There are groups of stones arranged exactly in the pattern of the great constellations in the night sky. We can see Orion, Leo and Cygnus. The Cygnus group has its central point at Traboe Cross, near Goonhilly, and this alignment is at 26 degrees east of north, pointing to the rising place of the Star Deneb.

On *The Lizard Peninsula* there are hundreds of standing stones. While we can see that some were used for indicating time, many others are part of a greater mystery. They were erected in groups in the shape of constellations that can be recognised as patterns of the figures of the zodiac. Even more amazing, they are in the order in which the sun passes through those constellations in the sky.

The first zodiac figure was discovered by Sheila in 1994. Leo was recorded in her book *Cornwall's Landscape Lion*. Little did she think then that this was the beginning of the discovery of a complete Landscape Zodiac, comparable with the Glastonbury zodiac in which she was born.

The Lizard zodiac figures are contained in an ellipse nine miles long and six miles wide. In England, other Landscape Zodiacs are found at Kingston on Thames, Pendle in Cambridgeshire and in the Preseli Mountains of Wales.

We spent many happy hours in deckchairs on dark nights studying the stars and learning more about the universe. She told me about her childhood in Somerset and being born in the middle of the lion in the Glastonbury zodiac. I had become much involved in the study of local archaeology when a fascinating thing happened. We were looking at our old local maps and she noticed that some of the place names in the Cornish language had a reference to lions and kings and things like that. The top of the lion figure is the Lestowder; the crown of King Tudor, and then she slowly identified the outline of the figure of the lion. There were many features that just could not be coincidences. One group of six very small fields with Cornish stone hedges was the perfect outline of the claws on the lion's right front foot. The top of the lion's head was a short sharp spiky row of cliffs in the shape of the spikes on top of a crown. Obviously they were not man-made, but very conveniently made a good starting point for the crown on the lion's head, and the place name Lestowder. Teudar was the name of one of the very early local kings.

Having been born in the landscape lion in Somerset, she was now living in another landscape lion, in Cornwall. It's about three miles high and two miles wide. She wrote a full description of that discovery in *Cornwall's Landscape Lion*. There was a pause of a year in these discoveries and then the process started again and culminated with our work on the complete zodiac of animal figures. Whereas in Somerset they are in a circle, the Cornish zodiac is an ellipse and there are many surprising coincidences.

We worked happily together, fitting all the archaeological research in between the farm work and the business. I think it was because we had been working harmoniously together that she developed her trusting nature, which had been severely damaged at the end of her earlier marriage. She confided in me stories of her childhood and how she was born with the natural gift of clairvoyance. It was suppressed by her parents, and she didn't want people to know about, but she trusted me with her gift.

This came to the fore at the end of one day when we were sitting in the kitchen looking out over the woods. Sheila said to me: "Your father's here."

I said: "What do you mean?"

"He's standing there in the doorway."

"How do you know it's my father?"

"I just do and he looks like you. He's nodding and smiling and wearing a lovely blue suit."

My father had died about 20 years previously and I doubt if Sheila had ever seen him in a photograph. Most of our family pictures had been lost as we had moved about.

"He's holding a tea tray with a teapot and two cups and saucers. There's something else on the tray that I don't recognise. He's tilting the tray a little so that I can see it better. It looks like a pottery model of a lady wearing a bonnet and a crinoline dress. Your father is smiling and nodding."

"I know what that lady is."

Years ago, when my parents had retired, they moved to Highcliffe on Sea, into a pleasant bungalow near to the Dorset coast. I used to visit them quite often. In the afternoon I would sit in the conservatory with Mother. Father would usually be busy doing some DIY project outside. We would often talk about their life in times gone by and in her own way she would sometimes reminisce about her life in service. She would ask if I would like some tea and biscuits and then she would ring a little pottery bell that she had. It was made in the shape of a lady in a bonnet wearing a crinoline dress – and the skirt served as a little bell with the clapper inside.

My father would hear the tinkling of the bell as she rang for tea and would call out, "Would you like some tea my dear?"

"Yes please Charles and a few nice biscuits for Edward."

Then he would come in with that tray and all the items on it, including the crinoline lady bell.

So standing in that doorway father had appeared, to introduce himself to Sheila in a way that only I could possibly recognise. Then he smiled and nodded and quietly faded away; on that occasion he said nothing.

Sheila explained to me that when spirit people appear for the first time, they always say or do something that can identify themselves to the person they are visiting. That's why my father had the bell on the tray. Sheila had no idea what it was or why. From his appearance she thought it was my Father; that was aided by her natural clairvoyance. Only I knew what the bell was and how it identified him with certainty.

That was the first time that I was allowed to experience and share in her gift. Then she told me of many occasions when she had seen visitors as a child. When she had spoken about them, she was told to keep quiet and never mention such a thing so as not to frighten people. Her father had remained silent as he was aware of such a gift in his own childhood but it was kept a secret to his parents.

Then, in quite a remarkable way, I received the gift. I began to receive the same sort of visits from a relative of mine that had died a long time ago. The first time was amazing.

One week I had a very bad cold and it developed into catarrh, then I lost the hearing in my left ear. I went to the doctor and he gave me a decongestant medication, but the deafness didn't improve so he sent me to a hearing consultant at Treliske Hospital in Truro. After an examination, he said that he would have to operate in my ear to remove a blockage the following Monday. When I was in bed at home that night, I woke at 2.30am and saw Mother's cousin, Frederick, standing at the foot of our bed. I knew instantly that it was Cousin Frederick as I could recognise him from the thick round dark glasses that he always wore.

He spoke to me and said: "Edward, for that hearing problem in your left ear get some chewing gum," and then he faded away.

It was a surprise and a shock and I had to stop myself from bursting out laughing. I didn't know whether to wake Sheila or not, but I didn't, and in the morning I told her what had happened and she said: "You'd better get some chewing gum." So I went up into the newsagent's shop in St Keverne and bought my chewing gum. I don't think I'd had any for about forty years. By Thursday evening, the problem had gone and my hearing was normal. On Friday we had a visit from one of Sheila's friends who was a recently retired nurse tutor from Treliske Hospital and I told her the story. She explained that there are two sets of muscles connecting the jaw to the cranium and the hearing passage passes between them. If that passage was blocked, the continuous massage of chewing gum for 48 hours could have cleared away the blockage and make everything normal. I telephoned to cancel the operation.

After that appearance, my experience of

clairvoyance grew and Cousin Frederick appeared again at the same time of day on various occasions. Each time he gave me the solution to a technical problem. The next time was when we were designing the supports to go into the ceiling at Goonhilly Craft Centre, where we were planning to make a restaurant serving 50 people in the loft above the big room on the ground floor.

The supports had to be strong enough to support fifty people and yet thin enough to go inside the existing ceiling space. His suggestions were a great improvement on the plans from our design engineer. Frederick only came when I had a technical problem that I couldn't solve, even though I was well qualified and he had only worked in an iron casting works.

On another occasion we had made 1,000 litres of mead (honey wine) in one large container in the lower cool part of the winery building. One of the reasons that our mead was popular was that most customers thought it was the best flavour that you could buy. We used local honey and on the moors on The Lizard Peninsula, there was lots of gorse and heather and we also had plenty of honeysuckle in our hedges and that added beautiful flavour and fragrance to the honey – and to the mead. We used top quality ingredients and allowed the wine to clear naturally with a minimum of filtration. If mead is filtered very finely to make it appear bright and clear, it loses some of the flavour so we just had to wait for it to clear naturally. Some of the big commercial customers wanted it quickly so they got it quickly, but the flavour couldn't be so good.

On this occasion, we had this 1,000 litres of mead that wouldn't clear – the haziness is thousands of tiny particles of the tasty pollen. Frederick appeared and his advice was to try and give the 1,000 litre tank some very slight but continuous vibration.

I had a small electric drill that was only used for modelling work and when you hold it, it didn't seem to vibrate at all so you could be very accurate. I fastened this drill to the steel frame that held the big plastic tank and switched it on and left it running. The cellar was cold so the drill kept cool even though it was running continuously. We took samples very carefully every three days and found that it was clearing and by the end of two weeks we were able to siphon off about 700 litres. It was perfect and our customers were delighted.

When people came into the vineyard shop, where I offered tastes of our drinks, I asked them if they like mead, which is a traditional Cornish and Celtic drink. They frequently said no. But when I asked if they liked honey, they would often say yes. Then I would say, "Please have a taste of our mead," and they did and usually said it was beautiful. After I explained our natural process, they bought some.

Sometimes Sheila and I went to the church meetings at Trelowarren together and we saw many improvements in the condition of people attending the healing services. At one time there was a lot of pollen about and Sheila had a particularly bad attack of asthma. She told me that she had been having attacks of asthma since she was a small child and she lost many days at school because she had to stay in bed. She couldn't go out into the pollen-laden air in our woods.

I suggested that this condition might be helped if she joined in a healing service at Trelowarren, but she was very hostile to the idea. I have to admit that sometimes during the healing prayers some of the people who were asking for help did seem to become overwhelmed with feelings and fell down and rolled about on the floor, sometimes laughing or crying. Sheila was absolutely against the idea and the possibility that she might make a ridiculous display of herself in public.

The next time that we did go to Trelowarren together, she said that she didn't want to get involved and would sit right at the back and just enjoy singing the hymns. Reluctantly I went and sat on my own in the middle of the church, as I couldn't hear if I was any further back. At the end of the formal part of the service, the usual invitation was made for people who wished to ask for healing to come to the front and I was very surprised to see Sheila walking past me to the front.

There was a time of music and singing and prayer. I couldn't hear or see very well as I was a long way back from the groups of people round the big cross, so I moved out to see better. I was amazed to see her rolling about on the floor and laughing uncontrollably. There were two ladies kneeling on either side of her by her head and they seemed to be holding her and praying while there was singing and live music going on.

There seemed to be an ecstatic aura around the group of people and the cross and I think it went on for about three quarters of an hour. Then it all went very quiet and I could hear just one voice praying and giving thanks.

The congregation present then gradually moved away into the next room for refreshments and I went as well. After a while, Sheila came into the room, looking radiant. She came to me and said that she felt well but couldn't believe that she had become involved with the healing group and 'the performance'.

Then we went home and followed our normal

life on the farm. There was plenty of pollen about, particularly under all of our beech trees but Sheila seemed to be immune and has never suffered from severe asthma since.

Six months after the event, she decided to prove that she really was healed. She printed a leaflet and organised sponsorship to walk up Mount Snowdon in North Wales, a height of about 3,500 feet, to prove that her breathing and lungs were in good order. Our local doctor checked her over before she went. She suffers from fibromyalgia so she gets a lot of pain in her normal daily life.

She went to North Wales by train and stayed overnight. Then in the morning, taking a sandwich and a bottle of water, she walked. She needed to pause for an occasional rest and she saw a small steam train passing her with lots of passengers waving. Sometimes the mountain is hidden in cloud but on this day it was fine and sunny. She paused again for another rest, ate her sandwich and finished her water. She saw the little steam train coming down again, with the passengers waving. It had been two hours since it went up.

She started again and plodded all the way to the top and sat down in the Mountain Top Café. The only food they had left was one Cornish pasty. Her heavy swollen legs had survived the climb. She had done it and waited in glory for the train to come back so that she could have the luxury of the ride down. That was 15 years ago, and there has been no sign of that bad asthma returning yet. She finds smoke and strong fumes irritating but she has never been ill from asthma again. That was a wonderful healing and a wonderful climb.

Then we settled down to what to us was a normal life. We developed the vineyard and the orchard and the woods. The business of marketing our cider, wines and liqueurs grew and our Cornish Smugglers Liqueurs became popular. They were even sold in Fortnum & Mason at one time.

Sometimes, on dark nights, we spent many happy hours in deckchairs outside the vineyard shop. We were both interested in astronomy and we were in a perfect place for watching the sky. There were no street lamps and we couldn't even see the lights of our neighbour's farm across the valley.

We became good at identifying the constellations and the zodiac figures like Leo and Pisces. One small constellation is Columba, the dove. That was useful but it was our familiarity with Cygnus, the swan, that ultimately led us to identify that there was a complete zodiac in Cornwall.

Sheila was now painting seriously and she produced one beautiful set of pictures of which the whole designs were channelled from spirit. That little book was *Pictures from God*. We didn't work hard on the stories and the zodiac concept until we had a lovely surprise.

The landscape lion had company. We were looking at the plans of the farm one evening, thinking about the possibility of collecting sunlight for solar heating, and we just happened to notice something. We weren't looking for any zodiac shape or anything like that, Sheila shouted out, "It's a dove," and there it was. The actual outline of our farm fields inside the fields of the surrounding farms was just a plain dove and our farmhouse was in the middle of it. We were really amazed. The revelations seemed to have started again.

The next figure was introduced to us when we were out for a walk just for pleasure. We walked along the footpath that goes past the side of the Goonhilly Satellite Earth Station to an old standing stone known as Dry Tree, where four parishes meet. Then we continued and we came to an arrangement of Cornish hedges. The edges were overgrown with gorse and heather at that time of year but we stopped to investigate a little and we were surprised to see that the hedges formed a very roughly square enclosure – and it was full of sheep.

When we got home and looked at the big field

maps, we knew what we were looking for. We could see that the enclosure of sheep was part of the head and continued into the complete outline of a sheep. The foot of the lamb included the Saxon site of Erisey Barton. There is a vague story of the finding of a golden fleece there, but we didn't try to find out more. The fleece was said to have been brought to Cornwall by Joseph of Aramathia. On our next walk, we left the car at Traboe Cross, where the road from Helston meets the road to Kennack Sands and Kuggar. There is a large stone at Traboe Cross. We walked towards the south and as we went along we noticed that there was a Cornish hedge built more or less parallel to the road about 30 yards away. That seemed strange, and as we walked along we found three more big stones in the heather at the side of the road.

When we were back at the vineyard, we fished out the 20-inch maps again and we were soon able to see that there were in fact five stones in a line roughly aligned at 23 degrees east of north. Alexander Thom was a professor of engineering and in vacations took groups of students out for survey practical work. They were often surveying groups of archaeological stones and discovered many interesting relationships. He had found a similar line of stones near to the North Cornwall coast when he and his engineering students were on a surveying vacation. They had identified this alignment as being the neck of the swan in the constellation of Cygnus. From Traboe Cross, it is easy to see that the road from Helston to St Keverne passes through Traboe Cross and forms the outline of the wings of Cygnus, whereas the road to Kennack Sands is the neck and head. There is a pool at the side of the road where the eyes would be.

It was also obvious that our first assumption was wrong and the landscape lion centred on Porthallow Vineyard was not an isolated figure – could it be part of something greater? We knew that we were sitting in the dove, and as it was a cool evening we lit the wood-burning stove in the big kitchen and sat holding hands in the silence. We let our thoughts have their own way. We felt smothered in an atmosphere of magic. Silence was the only way. We were coming to the end of the winter.

Sheila's painting went on. After two small books, *The Landscape Lion* and the *Cornish Zodiac*, then after another period of painting, she produced *The Song of the Sun*, which I think is particularly beautiful and includes her own words, pictures and poetry. My own spiritual development proceeded slowly and I got to know a wider group of people with spiritual gifts in the development circle of a local spiritualist church. I found psychometry interesting. It is a method of mental concentration on an object belonging to someone else held in the hands. Information about the person and their activities can be received by holding their hands. I have to work hard at it but all of these things come naturally to Sheila who prefers to keep a low profile – particularly with church people. Once we heard a heated discussion going on and one phrase was, "We don't have angels in our church."

I was working in the vineyard shop one morning and I was probably out of sight as I was labelling. Sheila was arranging her books and paintings, which we sold in the shop. I heard the shop door open and the vicar came in and gave her a welcome. Then they sat down for a chat and I heard him say that he was so grateful at being able to visit her as she was the only person in the parish to whom he could talk about the angels that he saw in church, and other spiritual matters. They talked and I remained hidden until he left.

Sometimes we shared spiritual experiences completely and at other times I didn't see the person that had appeared to her and she usually told me about the visit afterwards. Because of my visits to local spiritualist churches in West Cornwall, and there were five within half an hour's drive, I did see many mediums working and also went to some public demonstrations. I never met or saw anyone with the same gift as Sheila. Her gifts had been inherited from her family and seemed to have been passed to me in some sort of way.

Every medium that I saw passed on information that they received from the afterlife to someone in this life who wanted to hear it. They usually wanted to know if a relative who had died was well. Sheila receives visits from actual people in the spirit world, not necessarily from relatives. They speak to her normally and usually look exactly as they did when they were alive here, but seem to be able to choose whichever clothes they want to. Their age and bodily appearance appears to be whatever they choose.

I don't intend to write very much more, but now that I am 85 I think it's best to record what I do know before it's too late.

One personal spiritual experience that I will describe concerns my grandson, Lee Wesley Jeffries. He died recently on my birthday. He was a fine young man aged 29. He didn't smoke or drink and he was quite a good young builder. His hobbies were martial arts and bodybuilding. Sometimes we would work together on a building project that we were completing. We would get quite dusty during the day and after work change into fresh clothes. As it was lovely weather, we usually put on shorts – and then he looked quite different.

When you met him wearing normal clothes, with full-length sleeves, you might notice that he had a pretty little dragon tattooed on the inside of each wrist. When he was just wearing shorts and no shirt, you would see that he was tattooed on his waist, chest, back and shoulders. That doesn't appeal to me, but I never commented. One large dragonfly was quite lovely. He died when he was 29.

About four weeks after he died, he appeared to us standing very upright in a corner of the sitting room. He was just wearing a plain white robe. The top of the robe was open, showing his chest and his skin clear of tattoos. All he said was, "Grandpa, I'm glad I haven't got all those tattoos any more," and then he slowly faded away. This appearance of Lee seems to show that we pass into the afterlife with a body looking the same as the one we have now, but the skin is pure and unblemished.

I miss him tremendously. My son Mark, his father, died two years before he did, so Lee and I became closer and often worked together. Sometimes I wear his blue promotional t-shirt, which has his name and some building tools printed on it. My memories of him are good.

Chapter 7

Moving And Publishing

Work at the vineyard had become harder. Increasingly, arthritis in my left knee had made it more difficult to move barrels, lift boxes of wine and drive and deliver to shops where the boxes had to be carried a distance.

At the hospital, they had decided to replace my left knee. That one was probably worn quite a lot as it was the one I used to kneel on when I was shovelling on the coalface. We had to work kneeling as the coal seam was only three feet high. Bits of coal and grit used to get inside your trousers and could be felt stuck behind your knee pads and grinding in the thin skin on the knee, making it very sore by the end of the shift.

The surgeon's decision was to start with an arthroscopy. This involved making a small keyhole on each side of the knee and putting a camera in one side while, in the other side, a scalpel was inserted so that the kneecap could be examined and scraped in order to decide the next move.

Unfortunately, after that minor operation, the knee was covered up again but within days my lower left leg was showing red, green and purple colours as it was going septic. The knee was cleaned up again and I had lots of antibiotics until the infection was stopped.

Then the surgeon apologised for the situation and explained that he couldn't consider the knee replacement for at least 18 months as the leg bone was a big bone and there had to be absolutely no infection left in it before another operation, otherwise we may lose the leg. So I worked on crutches for the next 18 months while tests were made every three months.

Then my left knee was replaced and the decision was made to sell Porthallow Vineyard. I had been there for 25 years. We thought that the sale might take a long time as the property business was not good, but within five days a couple from London came to see the place and fell in love with our location, the beach, cliffs and views for about 50 miles along the coast to Devon. They had the cash and the deal was signed while I was still in hospital.

Meanwhile, Sheila was in Somerset visiting cousins near Charlton Mackrell, where she was born. She telephoned me to say that the bungalow that her parents had built, where she spent many happy years and where she still knew lots of people, was for sale and could we come and live here. So here we are at a different farm; I have come to live in Somerset.

The owners were selling this place as they wanted more land for their horses. The whole place had been neglected and all the lovely flowers and rose bushes had been eaten by their horses. It wasn't like she remembered from childhood, so Sheila worked really hard at creative gardening and has made it lovely with landscaping, lots of specimen trees, flowers and rose bushes.

We have restored the ancient stream, which had been filled in as the horses liked to roll in it, but the red clay bottom got into their coats and it took a long time to clean them for showing.

Then suddenly she said: "I haven't written anything for three years and my head is full of books." So she stopped gardening and started writing.

She was disappointed to find out that publishers don't accept unsolicited manuscripts anymore, her literary agent had died, and the publisher that had printed her books since she was 12 had been absorbed into Penguin so she had no contacts.

She became very disheartened at her lack of success in finding a new agent and another publisher but she pressed on with the discipline of four hours writing a day for her new book. This was a book entitled *Solomon's Tale*, a story of a relationship between a cat (our cat Solomon) and a family that he was helping in times of trouble. This book was the first that she had written which mentioned our spiritual life.

When she had finished writing and the manuscript was being typed to publishing standards, she was still very worried about having neither agent nor publisher. As I had given up my business in Cornwall and really had very little to do here, I suggested to Sheila that she concentrated on writing and I would take on the responsibility of finding out about publishing. She thought about it for three weeks before saying yes.

I am experienced in market research and I had read *Solomon's Tale* six times in manuscript, before it was typed, and I loved it. It was plain to me that the target market for this book was to cat lovers so I started to identify the market and its communications. There didn't seem to be any publishers that particularly specialised in cat books. There are two cat magazines in the UK and there seemed to be a big one in the USA, *Cat Fancy*, with a paid circulation of about 220,000 people. In the UK there are also lots of cat protection societies, all voluntary, and with their own small publications.

I did some research on book distribution and asked cat owners where they shopped. In general, their replies were, almost every week in shops for cat food and other products and about once a year in bookshops.

In the USA there is also one purely online cat magazine with about 7,000 readers.

So the conventional publishing and book distribution system did not seem to be right for Solomon. After some discussion, we decided on self-publishing. Sheila was against the idea from the start as in her mind it was vanity publishing but times have changed a lot. One of the most successful writers in the world has been Louise Hay, who couldn't get a publisher for her first book so she started self-publishing on her own and that book has sold 40 million copies worldwide.

We agreed on self-publishing, which I would finance. Sheila has been involved in all the discussions with the publisher and I have organised all the advertising, including printed and online publishing in the USA. Sheila puts in her own promotional work with Twitter and Facebook, which I couldn't do. All in all things are going rather well. A well-known literary agent saw *Solomon's Tale* and liked it. She is now Sheila's agent and has sold the translation and publishing rights in Germany and France.

Now the pattern has changed. The publishers in Germany are pressing for the sequel. Sheila is busy writing, which is one of her natural creative gifts, while I am busy getting this, my first and only book, organised. I have learned a lot from helping Sheila to have *Solomon's Tale* published. I'm learning a surprising amount from seeing the skill and care that she is putting into her work with Twitter and Facebook and how valuable they are in developing contacts with other writers all over the world.

I had to start learning how to use a computer when I began to be involved in publishing six months ago. I shall try and learn from her experience when this is published in a few months time. In the meantime, I'd better get on with explaining a little more excitement.

Chapter 8

Romans

On this farm, I still have a big area of grass to mow. We have converted a derelict part of the old orchard into a certificated location for five caravans, so there's about an acre of grass to mow there. Then there are the paths along each side of Monty's Stream. Sheila's parents, Monty and Kate, bought this six acres of land in 1962 because the stream here was just what he wanted for his retirement idea, to have a go at breeding trout. It comes from a round spring and flows all the year round at a constant temperature of 8 degrees celsius, which is ideal for breeding fish. It is a stream with an interesting past. The water has been tested and its quality is up to drinking water standards. It flows out of the end of our land into the beginning of the drainage system created for the low-lying land known as the Somerset Levels.

In the next field, it is close to the remains of a roman villa and other buildings. Amongst the relics found were pieces of leather items of clothing and weapons so it was assumed to have been the centre of a small group of Romans who were here to supervise the farming.

Grain was grown here and exported to Rome. In Roman times, there were two small ports on the River Parrott, which were in contact with Rome.

In the central floor of the Roman villa was a beautiful mosaic floor picture depicting Bacchus and his lover Ariadne – the Roman gods of wine, health and happiness. Grapes and hops are growing wild in the hedges here, suggesting that life in the villa would include conviviality. The spring of pure water was clearly an important factor in the location of a place to live. When the county archaeologists had completed their survey of the site of the Roman villa, they continued to dig in the centre of the foundations and found evidence of five centuries of Iron Age dwelling before the Romans. Visiting clairvoyants have seen the figures of Roman soldiers standing by the spring at night.

We drink the water, eat the watercress that grows wild here and bathe our feet in the warm water, which is a very soothing experience. Apparently this stream was known for years as a healing stream but the use of it was banned in Victorian times.

So Monty and Kate bought this land with the intention of breeding trout. This was before the fish were factory farmed and available in supermarkets. Their business was successful and in accordance with the planning regulations at that time, which said that if you ran a viable agricultural business on the land for three years you would be permitted to build a home for yourself on it. So they did. Sheila enjoyed living here and, as the big house next door had a riding stables, she taught youngsters how to ride and really enjoyed leading groups of riders across the Somerset Levels.

Monty died in 1982 and the place has changed hands a few times. When we came here, I was still in crutches so I pottered about while Sheila made a real start on making the property lovely. Time has passed and she is busily writing again.

A short while ago, on a Sunday afternoon, I was on my trusty Leyland tractor, mowing the grass paths in the field where Monty her father had set up his trout breeding enterprise in 1963, using this pure and constant warm stream. I was mowing quite normally and keeping the wheels about a foot from the edge of the bank when suddenly the bank began to collapse and slide into the stream, taking the right-hand side tractor wheels with it. We were tipping over and my instinct was to start getting off.

About 40 years ago, I was involved in the design and testing of safety frames, or roll bars, for tractors, and we soon discovered that in the event of accidents the golden rule was – keep holding the steering wheel. If you tried to get off, you were likely to fall and break some limbs at least. If you held onto the steering wheel, the safety frame would do its job and save you from hitting the ground.

I don't think I was musing about the Romans or anything else distracting while I was mowing the grass path by the stream. I was careful not to get close to the edge of the grass bank but suddenly the tractor started to tip sideways. The whole grass bank had started to give way and slide into the stream. In hindsight, I realise that we had had a lot of rain for a few days and although our land is well drained it was probably sodden.

The tractor and I were rolling into the stream and instinctively I started to try and get off. Because of how the controls are located, it has never been easy to get on and off and I usually have to swing my leg up over the steering wheel.

Then I had a momentary vision. It was very sudden and brief. Cousin Frederick's face, with those unforgettable thick glasses on, flashed in front of my face and he shouted, "Edward. Hold tight on to the steering wheel." So automatically I did hold tight. It is a difficult thing to do when your mind tells you to get off.

The tractor rolled over about 50 degrees and then the frame hit the other bank and then my head hit the safety frame, which is thick tubular steel. I was still in the seat, gripping the wheel.

The rear wheels were still turning and throwing up mud. The mower was buzzing and the engine was roaring. I had pushed my foot down on the accelerator pedal and I slowly realised that the accident was over and I was OK, with nothing broken.

I strained forward and pulled the button that stopped the engine. There was silence except the bubbling of the stream just below me. I sat there quietly but very uncomfortably. I seemed to have pain everywhere. My arms and shoulders were hurting from fiercely grabbing the steering wheel. I realised that no-one knew that I was there so I would have to climb out, but which way? I decided to sit quietly for a little longer and just breathe. Nothing was going to happen. I knew from my previous work in the Mines Rescue Team that people often suffered shock after an accident so I wasn't surprised when I started to shake and shiver and cry. I just tried to stay there and breathe deeply in the quiet air and sunshine.

It did hurt my ribs when I breathed in deeply but I started to look round and be thankful that nothing worse had happened. I had to think out how I could get out. I could see the water just below but the left-hand side of the tractor was still over the dry path. Even though it looked the hardest way, that was the way to go. I had to pull my right leg up until I could get my foot on the seat. Then I had to lean on the left side of the safety frame and shuffle my leg up to the seat a bit at a time.

I slowly pushed my body up while holding onto the frame until my legs could move over the side of the tractor and be slowly lowered to the ground, while I held on with the weight of my body. I was about four feet above the ground and had to take my weight on my arms and shoulders, which had been strained. It was a slow and painful move but eventually my boots touched the ground, then I let go and collapsed in a heap.

Ever since the operation, my left knee has been weak and my right foot has some internal bones missing, so balance is not easy. I normally have difficulty getting up if I fall down. I did manage to roll over, and by getting my hands on the big rear wheel of the tractor, pull myself up onto my knees.

Then it was another heave to get up onto my feet.

Not far away there were some bamboo canes holding a guard round a newly planted tree in place so I was able to get two of those and start to shuffle the half mile home with those bendy canes helping just a little.

I was very grateful to reach the stone seat that we have built round the source of the stream where I sat. I would have dearly liked to put my hands and feet into the water. The seat felt like a very safe place, and a good place from which to offer prayers of gratitude. I am amazed that Cousin Frederick was there but that must be something I'll have to learn about in the afterlife and what I'll do there.

I thought that I had finished writing my memories of spiritual events that have happened to me, but as I was doing my final checking, I remembered another occasion. It had nothing to do with miracles or clairvoyance or healing, but as it was the first time anything happened to me indicating an awareness of another level of living, I will include it. Another reason for including it is the funny and humiliating ending.

After university I occasionally had free time in which I helped a small engineering company with their marketing. It was this company that produced the tractor roll bars that were tested at Cranfield. One year they exhibited their products, which were all in the agricultural field, at an exhibition designed to promote exports. They took a number of orders to be delivered to farms in France. As I spoke a certain amount of French, I agreed to deliver them, so they hired a lorry and loaded it. They booked it onto a ferry to Cherbourg, so I drove to Devon and then took the lorry to France.

From Cherbourg, I started to drive south. When it began to get dark, I turned off left to try and find a place to park by the seaside. I did and had my supper and stretched out my sleeping bag across the seats. I soon went to sleep but in the night I was awakened by an almighty crash and continuous loud noises and sharp bangs. It was really terrifying and must have lasted about half an hour. I peeped out but there were no lights or flashes to be seen. When it stopped, I felt quite breathless but I did go to sleep again. In daylight I got up and walked around and saw that I had parked in a wide piece of the road by the beach. There appeared to be the remains of old lorries sticking up out of the sand. I think I might have heard sounds left over from the D-Day battle all those years ago. When I got home again, I looked at an up-to-date map and saw that where I had stopped was called Omaha beach.

I had my breakfast and went on my way with my maps to find my first farm customers. They thought it quite comical that a young Englishman was delivering their goods. Eventually, I found my last place to deliver. It was quite a large sheep farm on an elegant estate. As there were a lot of gates and pieces to be fitted together, they invited me to stay in their house and we could unload and assemble everything in the morning. I think the breed of sheep was Charollais. They looked somehow different from ours.

In the morning, we unloaded the equipment and fitted it all together. It was named a 'Flockmaster' and had an ingenious arrangement of fences and gates in which to drive the flock and there were small swinging gates to separate the sheep as required.

The owners of the estate had invited a number of their neighbouring farmers to see the demonstration. The flock of sheep were driven into place and then the small gates were operated, but their sheep were having none of this. Then I could see the difference between those sheep and ours. Their legs were considerably longer, so instead of going through the swinging gates, they just jumped over the side panels and ran off. The visiting farmers roared with laughter and some derision. I blushed and said nothing. The visitors drifted into the barn, which had been laid with wine and snacks. The estate owner, the prospective purchaser, slapped me on the shoulder and said in good English, "Come and have lunch in the house and I'll have it all put back on your truck while we're eating." I got back to Cherbourg next day and to Exmoor the day after.

Chapter 9

Reflections

How can my experiences be helpful to other people?
What have I learned?

Afterlife

I have learned for certain that the afterlife exists and
our life continues after we die. The visitors that have
come to Sheila and I from the afterlife have been a
variety of relatives and many other people that we
have known. I had assumed that visits from people
now living in the afterlife would be for important
reasons. Sometimes the visits have been to give us
important information; at other times they have been
purely social. On occasion they have been to advise
us, showing that they have knowledge of events that
are still to happen.

Occasionally they have actually been helpful in healing us, whereas at other times healing has taken place apparently without any other person being involved. It has surprised me when the visits have been for trivial purposes, such as when my wife's mother popped into the kitchen to remind her to cut holes in the pastry on top of the blackberry and apple pie she was making.

Chapter 10

AA

When I became sober, I began attending meetings of Alcoholics Anonymous. I learned about their valuable twelve step programme. AA wasn't the power that helped me to stop drinking alcohol, but it certainly taught me how to live decently afterwards. I realised that all through my adult life I had been propped up by alcohol. My thinking and sense of values had been distorted. Directly and indirectly, I had hurt a lot of people. What really disturbs me now that I know about the afterlife is that I may well meet the people that I have hurt here again. That seems to be a very unpleasant prospect. No amount of lying or denial will get me out of that.

One of the suggestions in the AA programme is that when we are really sober, we should try to apologise and make amends to the people we have hurt. This sounded like a difficult and painful thing to do and I could sense the humiliation in meeting some of those people. I would tell them I wasn't drinking any more and I was now really aware of what I did and I wished to apologise and make appropriate amends, if they will let me.

Recovery

I did receive advice and support from a new friend who knew a lot about my past life.

I found the first people on my list and went to see them. I was frightened and ashamed, but when they understood that I really had stopped drinking, they were prepared to listen to me and then accept my apology and amends. When I left them, my fear had lessened and I was thankful for what I had done.

As time passed, I was able to find and meet others to whom I was able to apologise. I could see that I was building a group of people who I wasn't afraid of meeting again in this life or the next. It didn't always involve meeting people. When I had stolen money, I was sometimes able to pay it back and only God and I knew that I had done the best I could. That was one aspect of my new sober life that helped me to regain a bit of self-respect and reduce my guilt about my past.

When I think back over all those years, it seems strange that I had changed from a relatively quiet and harmless boy into a hardworking and well-educated but very devious and dishonest alcoholic young man. I think I can see now that selfishness was at the heart of much of my bad behaviour, which I had tried hard to conceal. I became more of a liar, trying to justify my behaviour to myself, and I had been driven by material objectives. I was not a good person.

Many times through the years, when I thought of the healing miracles that had happened to me, I wondered, "Why me?" I knew that I hadn't been a good person or done anything to earn those favours. I seemed to be very slow to learn the most obvious things. I realise now that not only has God shown His will for me to become sober and start to lose my selfishness and bad behaviour, he has also shown that He loves me.

That was a difficult thing for me to accept. As I realised what sort of person I had been, I wondered how anyone could have liked or loved me. Now, in order to help me explain how I am beginning to understand, I need to quote a short piece from the twelve steps book of Alcoholics Anonymous.

Step Eleven

"Sought through prayer and meditation to improve our conscious contact with God, as we understand Him, asking only for knowledge of His will for us and the ability to carry it out."

For many years, I have been asking to know God's will for me and I really thought I hadn't a clue. I had thought the only friends I had were my drinking friends in pubs. I had always looked forward to my first quick drink to start the process of changing my feelings of being a mouse to being John Wayne. I knew that the more I drank, the friendlier everyone seemed to become. As the appreciation of being sober and not having any desire for alcohol became more secure, I began to think more about my neighbours and other local people who had been so kind to me. In particular, about the neighbour who had come in the night to find me and take me to hospital when I was scalded but still drunk. His wife, who had cleaned up the house and brought me proper meals.

I thought particularly about the local couple who had taken me to the healing services at Trelowarren Chapel. It can't have been very pleasant for them coming into my home and taking me, a disgusting drunk, to that lovely place with many of their friends there. What on earth had they all thought of me? I know that my own instinctive reaction would be to turn my back on a drunk rather than try and befriend him, but they had done it. They had befriended me. I can feel the tears coming again as I write and remember those times and those people; they were very kind. Bill and Jenny knew that I was a drunk living in squalor, yet they came to find me and help me. They persuaded me to go to church with them. They must have known they were taking a risk. Drunks are unpredictable and often uncontrollable.

I must have stunk of booze in their car. What did their friends at Trelowarren think? Then the first visit was a failure. I just sat where I was put and didn't respond at all, but they didn't give up on me. They persevered to try and help me. Was that really a wonderful example of loving ones neighbours? I was soon about to learn.

My hobby is astronomy and I believe that the whole universe and everything in it was created by God and has continued to evolve. I had no idea what I am for or of God's will for me until yesterday. It happened at last night's AA meeting. After the meeting, I went to talk to a new member who was still struggling. In our conversation, he asked me how long I had been sober and I told him about 25 years.

Then he said, "I should think that God person is jolly pleased that you are still sober and a friendly useful chap now."

It was on the way home that the penny dropped and I realised that God had shown his will for me at that moment, in an instant, while I was hanging on to that big wooden cross. He took my addiction to alcohol away. It has never returned and I have gradually developed into a loving and useful human being. Now I know that His will is for me to be sober and to use my life as best I can to love other people and try to help them with their lives. It's taken me a long time to realise this, so I'd better get on with it.

Chapter 11

Mary. My reminder of loving.

A significant change in my life took place when I found a small plaster statue of Mary, the mother of Jesus, in a small box of my father's personal possessions. I put it on the shelf above my bed. It is my first sight in the morning and the last in the evening. That reminds me of her relationship with God.

When she was told that she may bear a God's child from the influence of the Holy Spirit, she agreed to do so. She was obedient and said, "I am thy servant." Then she loved the child that she was carrying and loved him in his youth and as a grown man. She supported him when he was teaching and she even stayed by him while he was being crucified. She loved Him all through his life and when I look at that small statue, I am reminded that she was a wonderful example of a loving person. That daily reminder of love is helpful to me, then I try and think of loving things that I can do today.

I used to have difficulty with the notion of loving myself but now that I recognise myself as one tiny piece of God's creation, it seems natural that I should try to help other people look after themselves too.

Afterword

I know now that the effect of these miracles and spiritual events has been to change my life and my outlook on personal relationships. I know that I might meet many people that I have related to in this life, so I try to be caring and kind.

I am reminded of the immortal words of Carl Gustav Jung. In answer to the question, "Do you believe in God?" he said:

"Do I believe in God? Do I believe in God?

No, I do not believe in God.

I *know* him."

One of the most interesting aspects of the appearance of visitors from the afterlife is that sometimes, after one appearance, they come back again with other people quite soon, perhaps fifteen or twenty minutes later, for some quite different purpose. We have experienced this on many occasions and they will be written about separately. I think the importance of this is that it shows that they haven't come very far, so possibly Heaven is not so far away.

Now that I know where I'm going after this life, I can concentrate on the way I live this one as well as I can.

If any readers of this book have experienced healing miracles and would like to help establish a record of these with me, please send me details in an email, saying if you wish to remain anonymous.

If there is a significant response within a year, we can put them on a list and publish them as *Modern Miracles* and I will contact you again.

I thought that I had finished, but as I write this very last page, I must say that today has been a wonderful day and I wish to record it for you to share.

This morning there was the funeral of a very dear friend of Sheila and I. Antoinette had been close and very kind, for many years. We couldn't attend her funeral because of illness and distance, so at lunchtime Sheila did what she likes to do to remember a friend. She picked red and yellow roses and then set off to walk quietly along our stream, sprinkling petals on the water as she walked along, symbolic of the lovely spirit that has passed away.

When she came back to the house, her face was shining.

She said: "It was such a beautiful surprise. Antoinette met me at the stream and walked all the way with me. She was wearing a most beautiful pale purple dress and looked quite radiant."

Sheila and I shared the beautiful feelings of happiness, contentment and graciousness all evening.

We were looking forward to a concert of Beethoven's 9th symphony on TV that evening. A few years ago, a dear friend, Barbara, who was a musician, had come to sit with us for a Beethoven concert on TV. She died three years ago after seven years of fighting carpal tunnel syndrome, leukaemia and then cancer. Barbara had been really ill at the time of our wedding so Antoinette had driven her all the way from Cornwall.

That evening, as we sat down to watch the Beethoven concert, Barbara and Antoinette came into the room and sat with us for the music. We enjoyed it together and then they went, leaving us with such feelings of joy.

During one interval, Barbara said: "Life is so wonderful now. I do wish I hadn't wasted all those years fighting cancer."

Goodnight.

I wish you well.

Edward Jeffries

Part Two

Or perhaps I should say, "continued" in July 2013

1. A review of the situation
2. The messages received from spirit explaining the reasons for the miracles and physical clairvoyance
3. Acceptance of the task and immediate arrangements to change the publishing plans.
4. The original purpose of the book
(a) Personal records for the family
(b) Then atheism emphasised the importance of the facts
(c) Knowledge of the afterlife
(d) Death and life for us
5. The new purpose of the book
6. Afterlife and its importance in crucifixion
7. The task of publishing
8. The afterlife and its importance in the Christian religion
9. Visitors and their knowledge
10. Afterword

Now what?

Chapter 1

A review of the situation

From the previous pages, the pages in the first book, you will have gained the impression that the book ended there. I thought that I had written enough to record the unusual things that had happened to me, leaving out a lot of the embarrassing behaviour in between.

This is how I came to be, how I am and my own feelings, now that I have added the second part to complete the book. I have accepted the challenge and started to plan publicising the reality of life after death in the afterlife or paradise or heaven or whatever the proper name is, if it has one! We will find out in due course. We do not need to know it now as long as people know what we are talking about, but it would be helpful to avoid confusion.

This section does repeat a little, for good reason.

My childhood had been relatively quiet. If anyone had asked me if I was happy, I think my answer would have been "Yes, I think so." Not that anyone did! I was an only child and lived in a council house among about 1000 others in the southern part of that big industrial city of Birmingham.

I went to the same school from the ages of 5 to 11, it was a 5 minute walk across the road. If my mother had been watching, she could have seen me all the way to school, but I expect before then my head would have been lost in the converging throng.

I don't remember anything happening that wasn't part of ordinary school life; one teacher had a mouse in a 2 storey cage. We had no field so played football in the playground all year round. After school we went home and then played in the cobbled street which was hell for ball games as they bounced in all directions.

One afternoon there was a great diversion and the whole school came out to look. The sky seemed to be filled by the huge grey shape of a Zeppelin airship that had flown from Germany. It moved slowly and quietly and we could see the engine's detail. When we went back into school, that was the sole topic of conversation for the rest of the day, and after school too! My father had an old brown picture postcard of a small aeroplane that had landed in a park in Birmingham in 1911. He pointed out which cap in the crowd was his.

Our youngster life changed when Britain became involved in war with Germany. All of the school children in the city were sent away to schools in the countryside, as the industrial cities were expected to be bombed by the Luftwaffe.

Whole schools were moved, that included all the pupils, most of the female staff, plus the male staff that were left after those who were fit and able joined the armed forces. We did take all our musical instruments.

We were dumped in quiet country schools that had also lost some of their staff as well. Headmasters seemed to disappear to become officers and sometimes visited us in their uniform. We went to Hinckley, a country town in Leicestershire. It had no factories but was close to a large complicated railway junction. I was put into a house where there was a boy of my own age, Peter. His father drove a shunting steam locomotive, sorting out trains on the railway junction. Sometimes, in the evenings, we went with him and climbed up onto the footplate, shovelled coal, pulled levers and just occasionally blew the whistle.

Then, one night, the whole railway junction area was bombed and destroyed and all of our school were moved to Bridgnorth in Shropshire. That school was a lovely old stone building with a big sports field. We spent a lot of time there playing cricket and once I actually scored more than 100 runs.

I was put into a small house, again with a boy of my own age, Jack. The town of Bridgnorth is built in two halves. High Town is on top of the cliff, about 400 feet high, which is one side of the River Severn and Low Town is built along the river banks and once was a bit of a port. There is a long road that winds about and joins the two half towns but there is also a direct water operated cliff railway with two carriages linked by wire ropes. When one goes down with its tank full of water, it pulls the other carriage up, with each carrying about 20 people. We used to go up and down there as well, but one day the rope broke and both carriages crashed to the bottom and people, including my friend's dad, were killed. We only found out when we got home from school. There was a small crowd outside Jack's house and when they saw him, they parted to let us in.

Jack's uncle was in the front room and he let Jack go into the back room, but kept me there.

Jack came back out to me and flung his arms round my shoulders blurting out, "Ted, my dad's dead. He's been killed on the cliff railway."

We hugged for a long time, then his mother came out to us and we all cried together.

His mother couldn't cope so I was moved again to a house where their boy had asthma and spent a long time in bed. He had herbal cigarettes and that's where I started to smoke. We soon got into tobacco, which we both enjoyed much more. I'm afraid I got into trouble again when we went down their garden and lit a small fire to roast some chestnuts. The fire got out of hand and their big shed was burned down. I was found another place. I don't think I was really evil, just lacking in role models and control. In the classroom one day, we lads decided to have a look at one of the girl's female parts. She was a redhead down there too, as we saw when we pulled her knickers down. There wasn't much to see!

When the war was over, we were back at school and I actually passed the University Entrance Exam. It was 1946 and demobilisation had started. 95% of the university places were reserved for people coming out of the services who had passed their entrance exam but gone straight into war. Only a few unpopular courses had room for 18 year old school leavers, so three of us from our school went into the honours degree course in the Department of Mining. The metal mining courses were full, so we went into coal to train as Mining Engineers. If we succeeded in the three year degree course, we had to get five years underground working experience before we could sit the Mine Managers Certificate examinations.

The ex-service officers brought their drinking habits with them; they could hold their alcohol, we couldn't so we used to get into more trouble. Our older ex-service friends had come to university with one objective, to work as hard as they could and get as well qualified as they could to get the best job they could in civilian life. Larking about and wasting time was out. We lads had to work hard to keep up with them, and it really did us good.

We had time for fun with jazz and jive on Saturday nights. The place was popular with local girls too. There was one small social advantage in being a mining student. On site we had a small underground experimental mine which we used for practice in mine surveying, ventilation and mine rescue. Young ladies at our Saturday night revels sometimes expressed an interest in seeing our mine. I had the keys and had placed a couple of blankets in a cosy spot and I did have interesting discussions with the occasional girl.

The years passed quickly, and I was quite a drinker by then. When I went out into the Great Hall to see the results of the degree examinations, I was a little late and from the back of the crowd I couldn't see my name at all, but it was there and I think you know the rest. I was headed for the coalface, shovelling and sweating and drinking beer in the evenings to make up the liquid content lost. Male voice choirs did me good as well. Singing too was thirsty work. We often worked seven days a week, so even if I had thought about church, there wouldn't have been time.

How things change!

Now there is time and I want more. My behaviour has changed from bad to good. When I recognised that my life had changed from bad to good, it was a wonderful feeling, but I still felt trapped by my own personality. Temptations were with me all the time. Then I realised the problem. Ages ago, when I had been a student, I read in a book by *Maslow* that we were in control of our own mind. That came as a shock to me. I thought that my mind was in control of me.

Maslow said that if we have thought or a temptation that we didn't want, we could tell our mind to get rid of it, BUT we must not leave a void, or it will come back. We must replace it by a thought or feeling that we do want.

That's what had happened to me. All the bad thoughts and influences had been pushed out in

Trelowarren Chapel and my mind had been left empty and the bad thoughts were coming back.

I remembered the words of Jesus when he was going to leave his disciples without him on earth. He said that they would not be left alone. Another comforter, the Holy Spirit, would come to take his place. He would be like Jesus and continue his ministry.

That's what I needed. At home I got on my knees and prayed for the Holy Spirit to come to me and fill my mind and take the place of all my long established bad thoughts, so that I could begin to think, speak and work as a christian. That is what happened.

It is now about 18 months since I started to write the book and it was completed and typed in about three months. I had been puzzled by those unusual happenings but it was all an aspect of life that I could understand but I could not understand why such wonderful things had happened to me.

I had seen and heard of other people being healed. When I received the gift of physical clairvoyance – in which you actually see the appearance of a visitor from the afterlife and they look as real and solid as they did when they lived here, that was something that I had never seen before. I was more puzzled than ever. "Why me?"

I experienced remarkable visits right from the beginning of this phase. The first was from my father, to my wife and I, as we sat looking out over the woods from our tiny kitchen. She saw him first and I was quite electrified when she said, "Your father's here." I looked to the doorway and there he stood.

After that one, I had a number of visits from my mother's cousin, Frederick, when I was alone and then more when we were together. All these visits increased my acceptance of our living in the life after death.

Transfiguration

Matthew 17. Ch 1 – 4. Jesus' transfiguration.

"His face shone like the sun and his garments became white as light. And behold there appeared to them Moses and Elijah talking with him. He was still speaking when lo a bright cloud overshadowed them and a voice from the cloud said, "This is my beloved Son, with whom I am well pleased; listen to him."

His face shone like the sun and his garments became white as light.

I have now received many Visitors from Heaven. I have also had more messages, mainly explaining the process of our death.

After the death of our physical body, our spirit

body, which has the same form as our physical body, begins to separate from it. Our Guardian Angel is present and watching carefully all the time. The connecting cord parts and our spirit body continues to separate until it is completely free from our dead physical body. It continues our life on earth. This is the important fact which we find difficult to believe. Heaven is here all round us. We can't see the spirit bodies unless we have the gift of clairvoyance and they also wish to appear to us.

Our spirit body remains living here on earth. Our spirit body is made of light of varying frequencies. It can control its own appearance to some extent.

All the blemishes on the outside layer, formerly our skin, are eliminated and disabilities are removed so that we are complete and perfect again. We live here in a state, which we refer to as *Heaven*. It is here all round the earth. People still living in the physical body, as I am while I'm writing, and you are while you are reading, cannot see the spirit bodies which are all around us as they are formed from a frequency of light, or radiation, which our physical eyes don't receive. We can only see spirit people if we have the gift of clairvoyance and if they wish to appear to us. Between themselves they communicate by thought. If they decide to be visible to us, they can communicate by sound as we normally do.

The spirit bodies of all the people that have lived in the physical state on earth are probably here. I only know a little about the life of spirit people in heaven, just what I have seen and just what I have been told in the morning messages.

There appear to be two different ways in which we separate from our dead physical body. As our physical body dies, our spirit begins to leave. We are the same appearance in spirit as we are now in our physical body.

As our spirit moves away, the connecting cord between physical and spirit bodies is parted and we are our own separate consciousness. Some people in spirit seem to be just able to move away from the body and continue what we would describe as a normal life. Going where they will and communicating with the spirit people that they meet. I think that if our death has been the usual process and not a sudden event, there are members of our family here waiting to meet us and welcome us and help us to get used to our new environment.

Sometimes, when the spirit body has separated, it moves away and seems to float away upwards, becoming smaller to see as it gets further away. It may appear to be crossing a bridge of golden light, but I don't know any more than that.

Our physical body, our tangible body is bones,

flesh and blood, our spirit body is the same shape but is formed in light. It seems that we will have the ability to control the frequency of our own light as the spirit visitors have been able to reduce the brightness of their shapes to appear natural to us. They also have the ability to change the brightness of their apparent clothes as Jesus did when his garments became white as light.

We have had occasions when a visitor has appeared with a normal head and arms but dressed in a white robe. When we were asked to describe who our visitor was, they were able to change their robes of light into what we would expect to see as normal clothes, a hat, a coat, trousers and shoes, all appearing as normal clothes to us. After death we sometimes see the spirit body in normal light, and then it changes into shining light, and sets off on a journey in the sky, looking smaller and smaller, until it disappears.

A month earlier I really had thought my book, my precious first book, to be finished and it was at the publishers being prepared for printing in a few weeks time. There had been a few unexpected delays and it had began to look as if the process, from start to finish with Matador, would take about 9 months compared with three months taken for producing Solomon's Tale for Sheila. I had started to make plans for advertising locally in Somerset, and also in

Ireland, where there was a strong interest by the Catholic press in this book about miracles. This all had to be postponed.

This clairvoyance of mine seemed to spark off another series of delays to publishing as they came from the world of spirit, and I was amazed again.

Chapter 2

Messages received from spirit

I hardly ever dream, perhaps once or twice a year, but I started waking up each morning with a freshly spoken message on my mind. This happened on five consecutive mornings and I wrote them down in my bedside book.

The first message was: -

"The healing of your broken neck was to demonstrate to you the power that is available from spirit."

The second message: -

"The healing of your alcoholic state was to restore you to strength in body and mind so that you can work."

The third message: -

"You were given the gift of physical clairvoyance in order that you will receive and see visitors from the afterlife and gradually become sure of the continuity of life after death."

The fourth message: -

"You have been given the same gifts of physical clairvoyance and creative writing that your wife was given at birth. We hope that you will receive these gifts for an understanding of the afterlife and will spread this knowledge worldwide."

The fifth message: -

"We are giving these gifts to you as you have shown that your behaviour can be changed from bad to good. You have a wide knowledge of international marketing and you are brave enough to carry on this work in spite of the criticism and ridicule that you will receive. You have free will. If you choose to accept this challenge, we will help you."

To spread the knowledge of life after death throughout the world. I will accept this task which will be to try and spread the knowledge of the continuity of life after death. It continues in the life of our spirit body and our life continues here on earth.

The Afterlife, Paradise or Heaven is here on earth. There is plenty of room for us on this planet. If all of the land area of the earth was populated, there would be less than three people per square kilometre.

This must be the ultimate answer to my requests in "Step Eleven", to know the will of God for me!

Chapter 3

Acceptance of the task

This week of messages has changed everything. They have come at a time when we had already decided to move house, so we would have less work to do in the large house and the six acres of land with water features, woodlands, orchards and a caravan park. We had both realised that we wished to use our time in the way that we chose, rather than being forced to use all our time and energy working for the property.

I certainly understood the messages and I am willing to accept the task and do it as well as I can. I think that my own new beliefs in the love for others that was shown by Jesus and the love and obedience that filled the life of His mother, Mary, are wonderful. I am doing all that I can to base my life on such love.

Jesus spoke of loving God, loving ourselves as children or creations of God, and of loving our neighbours as ourselves. Mary showed us love through her whole life. She accepted the role of Jesus' mother. She bore him and nurtured him and supported him through his life and ministry and even unto being present at his death through crucifixion.

She would have heard him say the words that he spoke to the second thief on the cross.

The thief said to Jesus, "Remember me when you come into your Kingdom."

Jesus replied, "Truly I say to you, *today* you shall be with me in Paradise."

Please pause to take in the full meaning of those words.

"TODAY" not when your bones have been in the ground for a thousand years.

TODAY. Was Jesus referring to life after death happening straight away?

"We are dying today and today we shall be together in Paradise."

WAS JESUS REFERRING TO LIFE AFTER DEATH AS THE CONTINUITY OF OUR LIFE IN SPIRIT?

I think he was, and so has every spirit visitor that has been to visit us to heal or inform, or to save, or just to share in our pleasure. Their visits have confirmed life after death.

I feel that now I know that life continues after death. I do not just *believe* it, I *know* it now.

That is the message I have to try and publicise.

I have had to delay the publishing of the book so that these chapters can be added and I think that will work. I had to argue about it but the publishers have now agreed to stop the progress on printing the book as they have it. I will complete these chapters which answer all the questions raised in the book and point the way forward.

When they receive these chapters, they will be edited, checked and typeset and work will start again. In the meantime, I will start to think and plan the promotion and I will try to obtain appropriate advice.

The Press Releases and the Advance Information will have to have a change of emphasis.

Now that the book has changed from just being a family record to basically a missionary document, I can feel what a change it has made for me. From messing about on the farm, without any real purpose, I am now a man with a job to do, and what a job! I suppose it's a happy coincidence that on Sunday and Monday, 24th and 25th July, at the inauguration of the new priest in charge at the local church in Compton Dundon, Somerset, one of the hymns that we sang with enthusiasm was 235:

"I the Lord of Sea and Sky. I have heard my people cry. All who dwell in dark and sin my hand will save."

Then, after each verse, we sang enthusiastically:
"Here I am Lord. Is it I Lord?
I have heard you calling in the night
I will go Lord if you lead me
I will hold your people in my heart."

What a lovely kind offer. I can imagine the reaction of God's voice, spoken from the roof to one of us singers, after the first line. Yes, it is you Jack, I'm glad that you will go, stay behind after church and when all the others have gone, I'll tell you where I want you to go. Thank you for your offer.

"I'm sorry, Lord, I didn't really mean it. It's just a hymn that I enjoy singing."

Is that what the general response would be?

Chapter 4

The original purpose of this book

(a) Personal records for the family

The original purpose of Miracles and Visitors from the Afterlife was to make a record of the unusual events that had happened to me; the healing of my neck, the healing from alcoholism and the healing of my wife's asthma.

Then the other events that were unusual to me were the events related to physical clairvoyance and actually 'writing'.

The appearance of my father and then various visits by my cousin Frederick, with a cure for my deafness and, on another occasion, giving me advice on a building problem I had. Then, on another occasion, providing me with a solution to a cider problem I had. Then a further two more visits when he was involved in saving me in tractor accidents.

I was puzzled as to why these wonderful things had happened.

All of these events were unusual and my wife suggested I wrote them down for family interest.

(b)Atheism

While I was writing about those events, I became aware, in the course of normal conversations with friends at church, of the big push being made to promote atheism, particularly by a well-known academic writer, Professor Richard Dawkins, at Oxford. I read some of his books and although his writing is good and convincing – particularly to me, knowing nothing of religious or philosophy studies. It seemed to wander over many religious concepts and said things about the origins of Christianity that are not true. I was struck by the absence of facts and evidence.

I then read books by two other professors, Keith Ward and Alister McGrath. They are acknowledged in their fields of philosophy and religious studies. They disagreed with some of the conclusions drawn by Richard Dawkins on lack of evidence. Richard Dawkins doctorate related to an intensive analysis of the relevance of pecking order in chickens: – Ph.D.

One chapter in Keith Wards book, *Pascal's Fire*, concentrated on a review of miracles and the importance of reliable witnesses and the difficulty in finding them. I realised that many of the things that had happened to me were actually facts, and some people would describe them as miracles. I am still alive and there are witnesses to all the things that happened, so that might be useful as facts. I have been told in one of the morning messages that when our physical body dies, our spirit body remains, showing the same identity and having the same consciousness. Any visible defects, blemishes, disabilities or tattoos are removed. We do not change our form. If there has been true love between people in the physical world, it remains in spirit life.

What we refer to as 'Heaven' or the 'Afterlife', is the spiritual aspect of this physical world in which we live now. We do not go there, we are there. We cannot see the people living there now unless we have the gift of clairvoyance.

Death is not a tragedy to those who die. They have already found themselves in a new life of beauty and joy. If you loved them, you will be with them again.

(c) Knowledge of the afterlife

When Jesus was being crucified with two thieves, one said to Jesus, "Jesus remember me when you come into your Kingdom." Jesus said to him, "Truly, I say to you, today you shall be with me in paradise."

This is quoted from the gospel according to Luke, Ch 23, v 42 – 43.

Jesus is saying to the thief that after they die that day, they will both be in paradise that same day. I am taking the word 'paradise' to have the same meaning as heaven or the afterlife.

In our own experiences with visitors from the afterlife, there have been two occasions when the visitor has come to us during their own funeral service. On one occasion, I know that the coffin had been buried and the congregation had returned into the church to complete the service. When the service was over and people were leaving the church, the lady whose body had been buried in the coffin appeared to us in the church. She looked fine and was wearing a full length green dress. She spoke about our clairvoyance. I think she said "I see that you both have the gift now." Looking at my wife she said, "You can use your gift now my dear." This was the lady that had forbidden the young girl to say what she saw. "You'll only frighten people!" Then she faded away.

On the other occasion, the funeral was in Devon but we couldn't go and whilst we were thinking of Antoinette, she 'came' to us at home and walked alongside the stream as rose petals were being floated in memory of her. I do not know the details of the service, but it was that morning.

When my grandson, Lee, died, I was with him for about 5 hours in Treliske Hospital, holding his hand and watching the blood pressure indicators slowly approach zero. I held his hand for a long time and kept talking gently to him. I told him of my love for him and of my gratitude for knowing him and of the pleasure that I had had working with him.

Two doctors came and examined him and told me that his life had ended. We had a brief discussion about organ donation of which I approve. Then they explained that they would have to keep the life support machine operating for the benefit of the organs, so I would have to leave now as they would be examining his body again and starting the procedure for the organ replacement process. When it was completed, the hospital would write to confirm the details.

His body had still not been buried as it was in the care of the coroner while an inquest was being held. Lee came to us about 200 miles from where his body lay, to show us his new, clean, pink chest skin, with no tattoos. All he said was "Grandpa, I'm glad that I don't have tattoos anymore!"

Between us, we have had hundreds of visits in many ways and in many places. Sometimes people come on their own, sometimes in pairs, sometimes in a group of 10 or so, and sometimes a whole roomful – perhaps 50.

I have absolutely no doubt that life continues after we have died. I don't just believe it, I *know* it!

Almost the same words were used by Carl Jung when Desmond Wilcox asked him, "Dr Jung, do you believe in God?" Jung replied, "No, I do not believe in God, I know him."

In the course of my own initial enquiries for this work, I have conducted research among a variety of local people. I prepared postcards with 3 questions with tick boxes.

The questions on one postcard were:

I do believe in God.   ☐
I do not believe in God.   ☐
I have no beliefs about a God.   ☐
Please tick one box.   ☑

Do not put your name on the card.
This is anonymous research.

The other postcard had 3 related questions: -

I do believe in life after death. ☐
I do not believe in life after death. ☐
I don't know. ☐
Please tick one box. ☑

Do not put your name on the card.
This is anonymous research.

The results were: -

Card one – 6% do believe in God, 10% do not believe in God and 84% didn't know.

Card two – 9% do believe in life after death, 20% do not believe in life after death and 71% didn't know.

I wonder what the result of a similar survey would be if undertaken when you have finished reading this book. I will explore the possibility of enclosing research cards within each book.

In the Anglican Communion Prayer it is stated: -

"Father we give you thanks and praise through your beloved Son Jesus Christ.

He put an end to death by dying for us:

and revealed the resurrection by rising to new life."

That is clear.

In the Collect, it refers to "Jesus Christ your Son our Lord *who is alive* and reigns with you."

That is clear.

From these quotations it does seem that members of the Anglican Church using these prayers are stating their belief in the continuity of life after death, so there should be no problem in accepting that visitors from the afterlife are more evidence to us of the existence of the afterlife and the reality of life after death.

I find it difficult to accept the statements in the same liturgy that: -

"He will come again in glory to judge the living and the dead." and "We look for the resurrection of the dead and the life of the world to come." Although I say it in the creed along with the congregation, I do not believe in the resurrection of the body.

Jesus told the second thief that they would both be alive again on the same day that they died, not that they would be resurrected at some date in the future. Three days after Jesus died, he chose to come back to living here on earth. He was first seen by Mary Magdalene. Mary, the mother of James, and the others with them told this to the apostles. But they did not believe. He appeared to his disciples many times, the first time being on the road to

Emmaus, a village about seven miles to Jerusalem. He went to stay with them and broke bread and gave it to them. Then he disappeared. The apostles got up and went to Jerusalem.

They found the Eleven and others assembled together and they told them that the Lord had risen and appeared to Simon, then he came into the room where his disciples were meeting, even though the doors were locked. Jesus himself stood among them and said, "Peace be with you."

He showed them his hands and feet and ate boiled fish with them. He stayed with them and talked to them, saying that they had witnessed his rising from the dead. Then he left them and was taken up to heaven.

There is no doubt that Jesus said and demonstrated that he would die and rise again to continue to lie again on the same day.

(John 20 v 19 – 20)

(d) Death and life for us

If we do accept that after our time of death in this world we are then alive in the afterlife, what are the implications for us? One of them is that it seems we will have the chance to meet people again that we knew in this earthly life. Some of the visitors that we have had were our friends when they lived and they came to visit us together.

I must add, from my own knowledge, our appearance as functional people in the next life may not always be immediately after we have died. I think it depends on how we die. If we die normally, I think the process is quick, but if we died in a serious accident, then there seems to be the facility for recuperation and dealing with the shock. For example, people dying quickly in an aeroplane accident may be completely disorientated and not know where they are or why. All those situations are taken care of until they can resume whatever their new life was to have been.

Another aspect of the reality of living a new life in the afterlife is that we may well meet people that we would rather not be seeing again. It may be that there are people that we have harmed or been unkind to when a face to face meeting, again in spirit, may lead to unpleasantness, perhaps requiring explanations, confessions or an apology. I do not know, but I think it is a possibility to be borne in mind.

It seems to add an element of commonsense to the summary of the law that Jesus gave when he was asked which of the commandments were most important. It is stated that our Lord Jesus Christ said:

"The first commandment is this:

The Lord our God is the only Lord.

You shall love the Lord your God with all your heart.

With all your soul and with all your mind and strength."

The second is this: -

"Love your neighbour as yourself."

When Jesus was asked, "Who is my neighbour?" he replied in a parable which meant that everyone else is our neighbour.

We may have problems with the concept of loving our self. If we think of ourselves as a creation of God, we can understand how right it is to look after this creation and not to harm ourselves, but to give proper care to our mind and body. In the current social atmosphere when there is considerable pollution in the media, our minds and those of our children may be exposed to violence and unclean thought.

We should consider seriously the harm that we can do to our brains and bodies by the excessive consumption of alcohol, food, unhealthy drinks, tobacco and drugs. We have created another social problem to consider. We are now aware of the damage that we can do to ourselves by excessive consumption. If we cause ourselves to be ill by excessive smoking or drinking etc., is it really the role of other people in a public funded NHS to treat us or shouldn't we make our own arrangements for private treatment for this damage that we have caused.

Is this the way we will look after God's creation? As we proceed in this life it can sometimes be helpful to think about our next life in the afterlife.

Knowledge that we continue to live after our death here is a great incentive to love our neighbours while we have the opportunity. To live this life as well as we can for the benefit of others. This may lead us to an intellectual awakening, so that we may be able to control our ego and strengthen the voice of our conscience.

The certainty of life after death can be the strongest factor in guiding us to choose to lead a worthwhile life here, always looking forward to the next life when we shall meet our dear friends again and possibly people who were not so dear.

Chapter 5

The new purpose of the book

The original purpose was to make a record of my unusual experiences for a family record. This rapidly changed when I started to be aware of the promotion of atheism. Some of my experiences may be described as miracles and I became aware of the importance of witnesses and their reliability. There are reliable witnesses to the healings that I have received.

I became increasingly puzzled as to why a lout like me should receive blessings.

The five messages from *spirit* explained that, and my world was turned upside down by the recognition that now the book had a totally different purpose and I had the responsibility to promote it as evidence of the afterlife, as widely as possible.

In order to do that, I must try and make it clear

to myself what Christianity has to say about the afterlife and where it fits in to the complete scene.

Christianity can be summarised as trying to live our lives in the way outlined by Jesus. He seemed to have a difficult time explaining it to the chief priests of the Jews and even to his own disciples. When questioned, he put it in a nutshell, by cutting down the great list of commandments to two. We have mentioned those and they are clearly fundamental principles that we need to live by.

The next major question would seem to be our beliefs in the relationship between life and death. I find the records of what Jesus said during his crucifixion, that he and the thief would be alive again on that same day when they died, seeming to be in conflict with other statements about his coming again sometime to judge the living and the dead. That implies that some will live and some will die and, in other parts of the Bible, it is suggested that after death our bones will remain just so until some resurrection day in the future. It is recorded in the Gospels that about 600 people saw and spoke to Jesus in the months that he stayed living on earth for the second time.

The message given to me was to make the afterlife more widely known. The words of Jesus on the cross were perfectly clear, so I am going to accept that as part of the message to be broadcast.

There is an afterlife, it is *Heaven*, and we proceed to live there after we die here. Jesus demonstrated it and the hundreds of visitors that we have received from the afterlife prove it to be the case now.

It hasn't been written about for approximately 2000 years, so it is not surprising that people are uncertain about it.

I believe it was the Emperor Constantine who accepted that Christian religions could be active in the Roman Empire, but his condition was that there would be no more preaching about life after death. He had discovered that he had no power over Christians when he threatened them with a punishment of death, so that was probably why we have not heard about it much through the ages.

The prominence of the afterlife does not really emerge until later in the book, so we may have to refer to it in our advertising and public relations efforts.

The prime purpose of the book now is to provide a great deal of evidence to prove the existence of the afterlife and its importance in the christian religion.

The state of the reference to life after death is not clear in the current christian liturgical statements. Most people seem to have the picture of bones lying here for centuries and then they may be magically formed into living people again, as celebrated in the spiritual song *Dry bones, Dry bones, Dem dry bones,* going to get up and walk. I do not think we believe that now. Our adoption of the Hindu system of cremation has put an end to that.

So, what do we have?

We have the statement of Jesus to the second thief, "Truly I say to you that we shall be in paradise today." That is a clear statement. We do not know about the thief, but we do know that Jesus was back after two more days, and was active with his friends and many crowds of people some time before proceeding to the afterlife again. While he was here for the second time, he was very busy. This is referred to in the last verse of the last chapter of John 21 v 25.

"There are also many things which Jesus did; were every one of them to be written, I suppose the world itself could not contain the books that would be filled."

Although the concept of life after death has been neglected and, as a result, Anglican Christianity is not now a major religion, having its foundation in the actions of the immoral murderings of Monarch Henry VIII, which got the Church of England off to a poor start as he plundered the country, destroying the monasteries and stealing their assets and killing thousands of monks, which became the foundation of the Church of England.

We have got to do better. Telling and living the truth and trying to live as christians. As Jesus told: "Love your God and love your neighbour as yourself.

So, our message has two prongs. There is an afterlife and that's where we go as soon as we die. One visitor gave us a very direct hint while she was visiting us.

She had died after a long fight against carpal tunnel syndrome, then arthritis and cancer, which spread all through her body. She kept fighting it but eventually lost her life. When she came here *visiting*, she said "Life in the afterlife is wonderful. I wish I hadn't wasted those 7 years fighting cancer."

Our life does not just cease so that we are no more. Funerals can have an element of sadness as, quite often, we do miss the person that has gone.

If we could see the whole picture we could have some real surprises. We have known the deceased person to be present during the funeral service – beautifully dressed and evidently joyful.

The afterlife is there, our friends are going there and I feel sure that the more open and honest we are about this possibility, the happier we will be in our life and the more sensible we will be about our death. Let's make our life a life to be proud of. Let's try to help God's purpose and bring more love and peace to the world.

R.I.P – No – now for an opportunity to live a kind and happy life and to be happy and busy in the life that continues after our bodily death.

I am sure that we will have a choice.

Visitors and an appraisal of their knowledge

Before we leave our developing knowledge of the afterlife, I will reflect again on some of the visits that have been mentioned earlier. Then we can look at each visit to examine the visitor and try to discover what they knew about us before they came.

1. My very first clairvoyant experience, my father came. Sheila saw him first and then told me that he was here. When I turned and looked I found out that I could also see him, as solid as he looked in the flesh. He looked very well. He was well dressed in clothes of our time and he was holding the tea tray in his hands as he often did at home.

He obviously knew where we were and he knew that Sheila had never met him, so he would need some special identification that couldn't be used by anyone else pretending to be him. On the tray were the usual cups and saucers and a small pottery model of a lady wearing a tilted hat and a crinoline dress.

Sheila didn't know what it was, but I did, and I explained it to her. The purpose of his visit was purely to introduce himself and provide evidence of afterlife. He had died about 40 years previously.

2. Cousin Frederick. He was my mother's cousin by adoption and was of a similar age to my mother. They had grown up together in the family. He lived at Great Bridge, between West Bromwich and Dudley. He had poor eyesight and was recognisable by his thick round glasses. He'd probably had little education and worked in the big ironworks opposite his home making big cast iron pipes. I had visited him with my mother and, while they talked, I played with his two daughters. He was certainly not a technical person when he was alive here. When he visited me, he always came with the solution to a technical problem that I had.

The first time he knew that I had deafness caused by catarrh and a hospital operation was planned. He knew how the situation could be cured. I woke at 1.30am and he was standing at the foot of my bed. He looked at me when I sat up and said, "Edward, for your hearing problem get some chewing gum." Then he faded away.

It seemed so ridiculous that I wanted to laugh but Sheila was asleep, so I decided to lie down again and tell her in the morning. When I told her she reacted very calmly and said, "Well, you'd better get some chewing gum." I went up to the newsagents shop in St. Keverne and bought chewing gum. That was on a Tuesday morning and my hearing was back to normal by the Thursday, at about 5pm.

Cousin Frederick appeared a second time with the solution to a design problem that we had for the floor of the new café upstairs. He knew that we had the problem and where the place was, Goonhilly. I imagine that he must have discussed it with experienced structural engineers in the afterlife and then was the messenger for the solution.

3. The third time that Cousin Frederick came was with the proposal for clearing the 1000 litres of good mead by settling it with very gentle vibration, which retained the flavour, whereas fine filtering would have taken most of it away. Again, the natural picture seems that he would have heard us discussing the problem while remaining invisible to us. He could then have discussed it with experts and appeared in a visit to pass on the recommendations.

4. Cousin Frederick appeared briefly at Redlake Farm in Somerset to remind me to hang on to the steering wheel while the tractor was falling over, to

permit the safety frame to do its work. He cannot have had any personal knowledge or experience and, although he may have been there, there was no time for consultations.

I am not sure as to whether I saw him or not in front of the tractor in Butter Meadow, Cornwall, when the dead tree branch trick was enacted. It may have been my mind playing wishful thinking. I'm sure there was some power at work that saved my arm and the other parts that the branch crashed through my arms without causing any damage. (Witnessed by Anthony Richards and his son, Simon, as well as my wife, Sheila.)

5. My grandson's appearance to show me his new skin and his spoken words of pleasure were a reflection of my thoughts, although I had never spoken them to him.

6. When the friends joined us to watch a Beethoven concert on television, they must have known it was going to happen. They were both lovers of his music and saw that we were going to watch the programme. Perhaps there is no TV in Heaven.

I have only had this gift of physical clairvoyance for a short while. Quite a sufficient time to convince me that the afterlife is there and many people we know are there now and taking an interest in what we are doing.

When children are born, they seem to recognise friends from the afterlife that they knew before they were born. Please don't distract them all the time with toys that they cannot see. Remember that for about their first year, their eyes can't focus on anything closer than about a metre. Don't drive away their friends too quickly. Let them have their spirit playmates and as soon as they can crawl they will be happy together. They can keep some of them all their life.

I would like to end with a final consideration of the words in which Jesus told us to love ourselves. That was a long time ago and, of course, it is still true. Our societies have developed in some parts of the world and now there is much institutional care possibly playing a larger role that personal care or loving ourselves personally.

We now have far more education and knowledge of the behaviours that are harming ourselves, instead of loving ourselves. When, in the full light of the knowledge of what harms our body, it is not christian behaviour to harm ourselves instead of loving ourselves. It is surely our own personal responsibility to take care of our bodies and minds when we know the effects of our behaviour.

When we consciously harm our bodies by taking an excess of alcohol, tobacco, food or drugs, it is surely our own responsibility to love our bodies and accept that responsibility to get ourselves healed. It is our responsibility to love ourselves and not to knowingly harm ourselves and expect someone else to accept the responsibility of healing us. We do need to think about God's love for us and how he would like us to live and take care of this world.

No more.

Over to you.

If you have got this far, do you think you could help in this work of publicising the afterlife and life after death.

Or could you advise me how I can do it better.

Also, if you have personal knowledge or experience of the afterlife, please contact me as we may be able to produce a more informative second edition.

Thanks.

Ted Jeffries